THE SOCIAL MEANING
OF SURGERY

THE SOCIAL MEANING
OF SURGERY

Nicholas J. Fox

OPEN UNIVERSITY PRESS
Milton Keynes · Philadelphia

Open University Press
Celtic Court
22 Ballmoor
Buckingham
MK18 1XW

and
1900 Frost Road, Suite 101
Bristol, PA 19007, USA

First Published 1992

British Library Cataloguing-in-Publication Data

Fox, Nicholas J.
    The social meaning of surgery.
    I. Title
    617

    ISBN 0–335–09943–2
    ISBN 0–335–09942–4 pbk

Library of Congress Cataloging-in-Publication Data

Fox, Nicholas J., 1952–
    The social meaning of surgery/Nicholas J. Fox.
        p.   cm.
    Includes bibliographical references and index.
    ISBN 0–335–09942–4 (paperback)   ISBN 0–335–09943–2 (hardback)
    1. Surgery – Social aspects.   I. Title.
    [DNLM: 1. Sociology.   2. Surgery.   WO 21 F793s]
    RD31.5.F69   1991
    306.4'61–dc20
    DNLM/DLC
    for Library of Congress   91–23985
                                                                CIP

Typeset by Type Study, Scarborough
Printed in Great Britain by
Biddles Ltd, Guildford and King's Lynn

CONTENTS

LIST OF FIGURES
AND TABLE

LIST OF ABBREVIATIONS

A & E	Accident and Emergency
DCS	Day Case Surgery
F	Fitness
I	Illness
IT(U)	Intensive Therapy (Unit)
OT	Operating Theatre Suite
NHS	National Health Service
SC	Sterile Corridor

PREFACE

Writing this book has reminded me of the days in the late 1980s when I was just beginning the field work on surgery, which after many tribulations I am now reporting. At that time I was lecturing part-time on an undergraduate course in visual anthropology. While I was advising students on projects which entailed a period of ethnographic observation of an own-culture setting – a cafe, a shop, a fitness centre or whatever, and then producing a short video documentary report – I was myself making my first tentative steps into the field, my pseudonymous 'General Hospital'.

It did not seem too difficult to do what I asked those students to do – to 'make strange' that which was familiar. The world of surgery often did seem very strange, and entering the closed spaces of the operating theatre had something of the feel of entering a world of ritual and mythology like the ones which appeared in the anthropology texts. I was also conscious of how visual were the events that I wished to record. Along with smell – a sense often omitted from ethnography – the visual does not necessarily translate easily into a written record, and I have often imagined the kind of visual ethnography of surgery which I should like to produce – something between 'Your Life in their Hands' and a piece of 'new journalism'. Certainly, both of those kinds of media are evocative, and I share Tyler's sentiment (1986) that ethnography should have evocation as its task.

Of course, I might not have obtained the data which I have recorded in the coming pages had I had a video camera in my hand. Surgeons like performing, and the TV journalists have realized this, filming in the operating theatre at the least hint of some great surgical breakthrough. The brilliant whites, the shining steel and the strange clothes make surgery a ready-made spectacle, with actors who are willing to act out their stereotypical roles. So perhaps it was just as well that I was instead the unobtrusive person in a corner, scribbling the occasional note, insignificant enough to allow the participants to get on with their everyday activities, which I was there to record and try to understand. For readers who are seeking a 'scientific' record, therefore I hope that this book can supply at least in part the kinds of analysis which will satisfy them. But for those who wish to get a 'feel' of what it is actually like in theatre, I also hope that I have evoked a little of the experience. For readers who know the operating theatre from professional duty, the object is to provide an oblique view, to help them see the reality that has become routine in a new light.

Something which may not come over in the text is how enjoyable and interesting it was to do the ethnographic observation of surgery, and in this respect the analogy with other-culture anthropology may fail, inasmuch as many practitioners of that discipline privately record the disagreeable aspects of field work while they publicly report a culture's structures or kin systems. Part of the enjoyment must rest with the people who I was observing, almost all of whom were encouraging and helpful. In particular my key informants, and even more particularly 'Dr J.', without whom I might not have been able to develop many elements of the data in this book. To all who must remain anonymous, thanks.

I suspect that acknowledgements have a complex significance in the relationships that are thereby claimed to a text, and maybe I should avoid them altogether for fear of implying that anyone else should share the blame for this work. However, I must mention a few names, all people who I assure the reader are beyond suspicion. Dr Judith Clark supervised the doctoral thesis which was the avatar of these pages, and her comments and support over the years was invaluable. Professor Margaret Stacey and Dr Paul Bellaby examined the thesis and encouraged me in developing it as a book, although I should add that the book is actually quite different from the thesis. Dr Richard Thorn and Helen Nicholson contributed in different ways to my recognition of the importance of structuralism and post-structuralist analysis to ethnography, while Jane Naish sowed the seeds of my interest in postmodern social theory, an interest which has strongly influenced the writing of this book, and my whole perspective on sociological analysis. Various people have heard bits of the ethnography at various meetings, and I would thank all for their comments, in particular the negative ones, which are often the most valuable in making one realize the limits of a text.

N.J.F.

INTRODUCTION

Surgery: an unexamined topic for sociology

This book is about the power of surgery to heal. It examines, in detail, the everyday practices of surgeons and the other members of the surgical team, in and around their sphere of activity: the operating theatre, its surrounding spaces, and the wards which accommodate surgical patients. The material which is to be presented derives from detailed observation and interviews conducted by the author in these surgical spaces during a prolonged period of fieldwork in a large English general hospital during the late 1980s.

Many texts have been written on the techniques of surgery. This is the first, however to address, not the physiological significance of the medical specialty of surgery as a form of health care, but the social aspects of what is Western medicine's most prestigious discipline. Surgery and surgeons are exemplars of medicine, and bearing in mind the imagery associated with Western health care, it might be argued that they are metonymic for Western medicine, that they stand for all that medicine as a whole claims for itself in terms of expertise and heroism. Some of the statistics of surgery demonstrate its significance as a form of medical healing in the West. In England and Wales during the year this research was conducted – 3 034 000 patients were treated as surgical in-patients, with a further 710 000 as day case patients. The waiting list for surgery stood at 656 000. Over 70 000 surgical beds were available in National Health Service (NHS) hospitals, and over five million people attended as new out-patients at surgical clinics (HMSO, 1988). The prestige associated with surgery in the public eye has long been recognized by the media (Karpf, 1988) with the success of both fictional and factual broadcasts and reporting of surgical enterprise. But this profile extends beyond the lay perception of the relative status of different medical specialties. One indicator of this prestige deriving from within the

United Kingdom medical profession is the league table of consultants holding distinction awards in the NHS. These financial awards are given to consultants throughout medicine on the recommendation of a committee of senior doctors reporting to the Department of Health. Although proportions of consultants in different specialties are published, the awards are confidential, and the individual consultant who receives an award (which is then held for life and can amount to a doubling of the basic consultant salary) is never identified. In 1985, 35.7 per cent of all British consultants held awards. But the breakdown by specialty indicates that in the pecking order surgery comes very high. Although nuclear medicine (a tiny specialty) tops the list with 63 per cent award holders, surgeons do well in the award stakes. Neurosurgery has a 58.7 per cent rate, with paediatric surgeons gaining 55.8 per cent. General surgery attracts a 49.6 per cent rate, cardio-thoracic 47.0 per cent, oral surgery 40.8 per cent and plastic surgery 39.8 per cent. Only orthopaedic surgery, with 35.2 per cent falls below the average, perhaps reflecting its hammer and chisel image. Anaesthetics fares poorly, suggesting that the glory does not rub off from their colleagues in the operating theatre (see Chapter 3 for more on the relationship between these specialties). It is also worth noting the specialties which fare worst in terms of awards: occupational medicine on 12.5 per cent, accident and emergency on 15.1 per cent, child psychiatry on 20.8 per cent and genito-urinary medicine on 22.2 per cent (Department of Health, 1985).

These figures make fascinating reading. Because surgery is a human activity, conducted by human actors in social contexts, it is not 'just' surgery, just a technical intervention. Nor can the social organization of surgery be discounted as a perhaps interesting but otherwise irrelevant issue when it comes to the business of actually doing surgical operations. This relationship between the technical and the social is important in two ways, both of which must be of interest, not only to a sociologist, but to anyone concerned with surgery, as practitioner or patient.

Any activity carried out by members of a society is available for interpretation by their fellows. Precisely what meaning is attached to a particular activity will depend on the social and historical contexts in which it is conducted, and the extent to which these meanings are shared may be more or less localized. Power, in the sense of authority, can be understood as the ability to determine what meanings are attached to activities. The authoritative source, who may be denoted as an 'expert' in some field or other, has power to define activities in particular ways, to expect others to accept this definition. Western societies have become more and more professionalized as areas of expertise have been carved out, and more and more 'experts' with their own authority have constituted themselves. Surgery is a technical area which is imbued by just such authority. So the first area of interest relates directly to the title of this book: what *is* the social meaning of surgery? Given that surgery is such a strong image, that it can stand in the popular imagination for all the achievements and techniques of Western medicine, one might expect these meanings to also be powerful. What effects might these social meanings have on those who come into contact with it, be they staff or patients? And how significant are these social meanings for the constitution of surgery's practitioners as prestigious, high-status members of the medical and the wider community?

The second way in which the social aspects of surgery can be significant for the technical process of doing surgery is more fundamental. The points made above could be understood as implying that the social processes associated with surgery, which will be discussed later, derive from the technicalities. But what if the techniques are themselves constituted, at least in part, as a result of social processes? For instance, that the technicalities of hygiene in operating theatres derive not only from practical or bacteriological considerations, but from very widely held discourses on purity and pollution which antedate any scientific knowledge of infection. This is an established perspective in sociological analysis. The sociology of scientific knowledge has found examples which suggest that scientific ideas can be understood in the context of social and historical processes and the dominant notions of the period in which the science was done. This need not be repeated here, but I am going to argue that social processes by which surgeons, anaesthetists and other groups involved in surgery such as hospital managers seek to constitute their work and confirm their authority are achieved in part through the technical procedures they adopt. To put it slightly differently, where technically there may be more than one way to do something, the way chosen will be that which enhances the social processes and in particular, the prestige of those with authority, rather than that which might appear the most 'rational' in the sense of economic or scientific efficiency.

Of course, the technique at the centre of the surgical enterprise is healing patients, of effecting some change that will be understood as leaving the patient in a better condition than prior to the surgical intervention. If the technologies available to surgeons, resection, anaesthesia and aseptic hygiene, are in part socially constituted, then so will this central objective of healing. So the social meaning of surgery will be extremely important for any surgical patient. Indeed as will be seen in Chapter 3, it may be a matter of life and death. It will not always be so drastic, but as will be seen, the uncomfortable business of having surgery may in part be due to the power struggles which are going on between parts of the surgical team. Sometimes there is no great consequence for patients, and the interest then is more abstracted, concerning an understanding of how a medical specialty constitutes itself as possessing and retaining its authority.

Why, if surgery is so important as a medical specialty, has it been virtually ignored by sociology? In the brief history of the sociology of health and illness (which is British sociology's most populated sub-discipline according to Claus (1982), the topic of surgery has remained largely unexamined. The reasons for this apparent gap invite examination, as medical sociologists have been enthusiastic contributors to what Strong (1979) called the 'academic encirclement' of medicine, with early studies of 'doctor–patient interaction' in general practice followed by sociological studies of many medical specialties from paediatrics to community medicine.

Some of these studies in the sociology of medicine which focused on specific medical specialties adopted interactionist and ethnomethodological perspectives on their subject matter (for example, Becker, 1961; Glaser and Strauss, 1970; M. Bloor, 1976; Stimson, 1976; Atkinson, 1981; Atkinson and Heath, 1981) and it is possible that this perspective (in which the subject matter is really no more than a vehicle for generalization about the rules women and men use during interactions – any setting will do) has resulted in a sense that everything there is to discover about medical interaction has been discovered, and that study of further settings, for instance those associated with surgery, will not elicit further insights. A move to policy-oriented research (sociology in medicine), and the relative availability of funding for social research in topics such as health behaviour as a consequence of concern with lifestyle factors in disease, drug use and more recently AIDS, may also have moved the focus away from the acute specialties within health care. The critiques of medicine as institution of social control (Zola, 1972; Illich, 1975) or of capitalist exploitation (Navarro, 1976, 1978, 1982; Doyal, 1979; Waitzkin, 1983) have identified an explosion of acute medicine including surgery as the reason why preventive health care is the Cinderella of health services in Western cultures; perhaps stimulating an ideological strand in many sociologists who consequently have sought to redress the balance in their contributions. Nor does surgery possess an 'obvious' link with mainstream sociological concepts – patient compliance, life events, gender and ethnicity, chronic and stigmatizing illness. With its apparent emphasis on anatomy, acute disease, and apparently clear prognosis, it may thus have appeared an unpromising area for sociological study. Foucault's (1976) observations upon the social determinants of Enlightenment medicine's decision to 'open up a few corpses' have as yet to generate a sociological study of surgery's basic science cousin, anatomy.

Feminist sociologies of health and healing, on the other hand, have not ignored acute medical services in their analyses, and have considered the growth of medicalization in areas of women's lives, in particular those concerned with reproduction (Macintyre, 1978; Oakley, 1980; Arney and Neill, 1982) or the particular consequences of medical authority for women (Emerson, 1970; Elston, 1977; Roberts, 1981; Graham, 1984), and in some of these studies surgery has tangential significance as a technique impinging on women. Other studies have considered the 'surgical personality', perhaps stimulated by the notion of the stereotypical autocratic surgeon of popular literature, and indeed the results of these studies support these popular images of surgeons as authoritarianism (Coser, 1958; Eisenberg et al., 1983) and right wing (Wakeford and Allery, 1986; Wakeford et al., 1986). But in these studies the social determinants of a surgeon's personality remain unexamined, and for the sociologist, the objective must be to try to identify how this surgical authority is constituted, and that of course, as was mentioned earlier, is a central focus of this book. Without examining these social roots of a phenomenon such as surgical authority, by accepting it as a given, leads to unthinking acceptance of other notions such as patient compliance. There is a mass of literature on patient compliance – 3200 articles appeared in learned medical journals between 1979 and 1985 (Trostle, 1988). The sociological critique of compliance is that it takes a medico-centric, and thus ideological, perspective upon the enhancement of the doctor–patient relationship: compliance is perceived as a positive trait, representing the degree to which patients fall in with the wishes of their doctors (Trostle, 1988, p. 1299). Consequently, in much of the empirical literature on surgical compliance, this ideological valuation of 'compliance' is not recognized as other than legitimate, and the attainment of increased compliance is seen by authors as being achieved by what amount to ploys by which patients are persuaded to see their forthcoming, clinically defined, treatment as desirable. Pre-surgical anxiety is a focus in a range of studies which conclude that it is undesirable on various clinical grounds: it affects post-operative anxiety (Johnston, 1980), adjustment to post-operative pain (Reynolds, 1978), consumption of analgesics (Ridgeway and Matthews, 1982; Weis, 1983), physiological measures of recovery (Andrew, 1970), and length of hospital stay (Matthews and Ridgeway, 1981). Some studies take into account the possibilities of variation in patient perception of surgery and thus a need to match anxiety reduction to personality type (Andrew, 1970; Hartsfield and Clopton, 1985; Kendall et al., 1979). McNeil et al. (1978, p. 1397), reporting with apparently unintentional irony, described how

> patients with 'operable' lung cancer . . . were quite adverse to taking risks involving the possibility of immediate death. These results emphasise the importance of choosing therapies not only on the basis of survival rates but also on . . . patient attitudes.

The question which remains unasked in these studies is why these patients are also not quite adverse at a more general level to a specialty which can offer such dangers. The focus on compliance decentres the field of study away from the surgeon and her/his authority. Some sociological studies have sought to address the question of surgical authority by considering processes of decision-making. Assessing the relative risks associated with hysterectomy, Travis (1985) concluded that the potential costs are high in relation to benefits of the procedure, and that decisions over whether the procedure is invoked in a case will depend upon the surgeon's evaluation of cancer risk at the expense of patient preference. Knafl and Burkett's work on orthopaedic surgery suggests that in what is a relatively routine sub-specialty, emphasis is placed upon the importance of developing sound clinical judgement of whether a case is appropriate for surgical or non-surgical disposal. In comparison with other sub-specialties in surgery, this emphasis on disposal judgement had the consequence of turning orthopaedic surgery from a technical enterprise into an esoteric arena of expertise (Burkett and Knafl, 1974; Knafl and Burkett, 1975).

Silverman's (1981) study of paediatric cardiac surgery compared consultations involving Down's syndrome children with non-Down's children, finding that while parents had little input in deciding for or against surgery in non-Down's children, parents of Down's children were offered a very high degree of choice of treatment. Consultants allowed perceived 'patient happiness' to be a significant determining factor in a group of children whose potential was perceived as limited by their genetic impairment. In Bloor's (1976) study of assessment of children for adeno-tonsillectomy, parents could influence decision-making by editing the history of their children's illness career which they provided to the specialist. But the clinicians had a strategy to maintain control: they would use a search technique to display 'relevant' information, or by hijacking the parental agenda, inhibiting discussion of treatment and invoking professional claims to expertise.

The suggestion raised by these studies is that surgical authority must be understood not as a once-and-for-all given, but something which is continually negotiated through social strategies in the interactions which go on in the daily surgical enterprise. This negotiated character to surgical authority can also be found in the few studies which have described the activities in operating theatres. Atkinson (1981) mentions, in relation to the problems of doing participant observation, some of the negotiations of roles between members of the surgical team, while Goffman (1961, pp. 116–131) provides a short ethnography of the interactions between junior and senior surgeons in a study of 'role distance'. Seniority was not, he found, asserted in a unidimensional manner. Junior surgeons would often be restive in their low status position, particularly as this would be played upon by nursing staff; they would distance themselves from their menial tasks, indulge in horseplay or play the jester. The senior surgeon would similarly distance himself (sic) from his role, making small jokes to reduce his apparent superiority. Goffman regarded these examples of role distancing as oiling the wheels of a stressful situation in which all are required to play a part despite manifest inequalities in status.

Another study which bears on this negotiation of rank within the specialty was conducted by Bosk (1979). Focusing on those incidents in which errors have been made in the conduct of surgery resulting in actual or potential iatrogenic morbidity or mortality, Bosk described the internal control procedures which detect, categorize and punish error. These take the form of routine informal audit by colleagues and the ceremonial occasions such as 'grand rounds' and morbidity/mortality conferences at which errors may be openly discussed. Errors are categorized according to a moral order, with the 'unforgivable error' being the one which offends the normative obligations of the professional. These internal control mechanisms were a factor in determining quality of care in a survey of surgery conducted by Flood and Scott (1978). Interestingly, in relation to the material reported here on the relations between management and surgeons, it was the extent of power wielded by the hospital's administrators which was the principal determinant of quality of care.

One study which has focused explicitly on the techniques of surgery was conducted by Katz (1984). Her ethnography of the operating room (theatre) bears immediately on the work reported here, although from a United States perspective. Using ideas of ritual from anthropology, Katz suggests that the rules of the operation contribute to a mental set in which staff behave dispassionately towards the body and its contents. Rituals exaggerate this discontinuity, they 'make salient the boundaries of categories' (Katz, 1984, p. 346); as such they serve to classify objects and events during periods of dangerous transition where there may be confusion between categories. Ritual in the operating room provides autonomy of action to participants by defining and implementing the limits of the system. The surgeon gains autonomy in the operating room only when all the rituals associated with becoming sterile have been completed – up to that point he (sic) is seriously restricted in activity. If rituals of handling sterile instruments are not followed, autonomy is restricted. What is of value in this study for the ethnography to be reported here, is the focus upon the technical processes of surgery, recognizing these techniques as not 'just' instrumental activities but also as discursive activities which constitute the social world of the surgical team, providing the connection between minute-to-minute activities in the operating room and the issues of authority and prestige.

While accepting the value of the study, I am disinclined to follow Katz down the avenue of ascribing ritual significance to the routines of the operating theatre, for three reasons. Firstly, such ascription ignores the discourse of the actors themselves, which surely is what the ethnographer should place at the centre of description. Secondly, it could suggest that one can distinguish routines which are 'ritual' because they possess symbolic and communicative functions from the merely 'routinized' behaviour that otherwise occurs in the operating room, and that there is some underlying and irreducible 'technical' rump of practices unaddressable by social analysis. How might the ethnographer draw this doubtful line? Finally, the use of the notion of 'ritual' fails to address the issue of who benefits from routines/ritual. Do auxiliaries or patients benefit? Katz seems to suggest that the benefit is universal, yet by not explicitly addressing the power relations within the operating room the discussion of 'autonomy' is unable to relate the detail of practices to the wider issue of the privilege and authority of the surgeon in relation both to the personnel in the operating room, in the hospital, and in society. For 'autonomy' read 'power'.

The intention of this review of the range of studies which have addressed aspects of surgery has been in part to demonstrate the need for an ethnographic handling of this clinical specialty. I have argued elsewhere (Fox, 1991) that it is through ethnography – that is the meticulous observation of a field setting, including gathering of data by interview and other techniques – that the sociologist can start to unravel the practices which together constitute the discourses by which a social enterprise is constituted, sustained and reproduced by social actors.

Social theory, particularly within anthropology, has recently been re-evaluating the nature of ethnographic writing, to acknowledge that an ethnography is a text, constructed for particular reasons, and with particular rules deriving from its constitution within the academic community as a form of knowledge by which social scientists come to 'know' the world. This debate is well, though critically, reviewed in Spencer (1989), while Atkinson's commentary (1990) emphasizes the need for reflexivity in the constitution of ethnographic accounts. The most cogent proposition of the form such a reflexive ethnography might take is outlined in Tyler (1986). He talks about constituting a 'fantasy' of a possible world, a 'poetics' in which the reader can capture some of the experience of the ethnographic setting. This perspective opposes the traditional view, in which an impersonal reporter makes claim to scientific truth, and in this I have tried to take the arguments for the former kind of ethnography on board, including the use in the text of 'I' as well as the more impersonal 'the researcher', to remind readers of the real person who gathered the data. Because I do not wish to imply a single 'social meaning of surgery', the final chapter is not a 'conclusion' but a 'commentary' in which some degree of a more dialogic approach has been attempted.

The theoretical position which I have sought to adopt in this study is a *post-structuralist* or *postmodern* one, which rejects the premises about the nature of 'society' adopted in functionalist and structuralist sociologies. It is not really necessary to go into this in detail now, as the practice of this form of analysis, and in particular the technique of *deconstruction* which focuses on paradoxes, contradictions and silences within discourse, can best be demonstrated by illustration. The postmodern position is that of Bourdieu (1986, 1990), Derrida (1978), Flax (1990), Foucault (1970, 1979, 1984) and to an extent Baudrillard (1988). It is an approach within social theory which regards power as a fragmentary rather than a unitary phenomenon, mediated by actors' access to what is accepted as knowledge in a social setting. Postmodernism elides any distinction between truth and ideology, and for that reason its analyses have an essentially local validity, which needs to be read in conjunction with the stated or implicit commitments of its authors. With its central interest in power, it is of course, most appropriate for a study of a topic such as surgery, which from a social point of view, cannot ignore the authority and prestige of its practitioners, and the powerlessness of its unconscious subjects. Postmodernism in this reading does not refer to a periodization of something 'after modernism' except that it is a rejection of modernist social theory with its commitments to truth, reason and progress (Flax, 1990, pp. 39–41).

The field setting

The observational and interview data reported throughout this study was gathered during an 18-month period in the late 1980s. The location for most of the research was the operating theatres and surgical departments of a large district general hospital serving an English city, the pseudonymous 'General' Hospital referred to throughout this study. All identifying characteristics have been disguised systematically throughout this study. In addition, a small amount of data reported here derived from periods of observation undertaken at two other large hospitals, one in the same city as General, known here as 'Western' Hospital, and the other, 'Saint's' Hospital, a teaching hospital in another English city, and from interviews from two members of staff at a nearby general hospital, 'Southern'. No comparisons between these settings has been attempted, as virtually all data in the study were derived from General Hospital, and it may be assumed except where otherwise stated that this was the field setting for the data reported. Nor is any additional claim to validity made as a consequence of gathering data from more than one hospital.

General Hospital is located at the edge of a city, but in fact serves a wide catchment area including a number of small towns and a substantial rural population. It possesses accident and emergency facilities, and is a regional burns centre, but obstetrics are conducted at Southern, a general hospital some five miles away in an adjoining district, while mental handicap and illness are treated at specialist hospitals within the district. Surgery at General was organized in a department of approximately a dozen consultants, with surgical specialties in thoracic, neurosurgery, oral, plastic, orthopaedic, surgical gastro-enterology and general surgery (which in the district was defined to include urology and vascular surgery).

During the period of the research a specialist day-case surgery unit (DCS) was opened at General Hospital (DCS is not regarded as a surgical specialty but as a particular option or model which may be adopted if deemed appropriate). When this study commenced, most surgery was being conducted at General Hospital according to a traditional model of admission the day previous to surgery, followed by a period of in-patient recovery. A small number of cases, principally in plastic and oral surgery were admitted as day cases, spending only a few hours in hospital. During the research period discussions on creating a designated DCS unit were completed, and a ward closed for refurbishment with the particular accoutrements needed for day-case nursing. One of the theatres in the twin suite used for thoracic surgery was re-designated as a theatre for DCS, with a consequent re-organization of surgical lists for those concerned, centralizing all DCS at General Hospital in a single location. The unit was commissioned towards the end of the 1980s and the researcher thus had an opportunity to study the social effects of this innovation.

Surgery at General takes place in ten operating theatres. These are organized into five operating suites of two theatres. The five suites are identified in this study by the names used by staff at General: Thoracic theatres; Neuro theatres; Plastic theatres; Theatres N (principally general surgery); and Theatres S (principally orthopaedic, and some general surgery). Pairs of theatres share some facilities such as instrument preparation areas and recovery rooms. The layout of these operating theatre suites (hereafter OT) is examined in great detail in Chapter 2. In addition to these ten theatres, there are two further operating spaces at General; one is attached to the endoscopy clinic in the department of thoracic surgery, close to thoracic theatres, and a third neuro-theatre which at the time of the study was not in regular use for financial reasons, but which, as will be seen, features in a particular episode reported in Chapter 3.

During the period of data collection, the entire range of surgery at General Hospital was observed, and all the OTs were visited at one time or another. The database upon which this ethnography is grounded comprises observations of 68 operations. All were 'elective', as opposed to operations conducted after admission via the accident and emergency (A & E) department, although a small number of operative procedures were conducted either as a consequence of an original admission through A&E for accidental injury, or as 'urgent' neurosurgery cases admitted directly from a clinic. The vast majority were called for admission from a waiting list. Some of the organizational arrangements concerning admissions are considered in Chapter 6. Because no gynaecology is conducted at General apart from terminations of pregnancy, five operations from a gynaecology list at Saint's Hospital are included in this ethnography. The researcher observed six ward rounds, one Intensive Therapy Unit (ITU) round. Interviews with 27 personnel were carried out, some pre-arranged, others the outcome of unplanned encounters in the OT rest room or in theatre itself. These interviews were recorded in shorthand. Minor conversations were recorded as soon as possible after they had occurred, usually within a few minutes. The slow pace of activity in the OT, coupled with the relative indifference of the actors to an outsider made it an ideal field setting to report in this way.

Doing ethnography on surgery

As the data described in this study indicate, the researcher had, during the period of study, access to all the surgical spaces at General Hospital, including operating theatres and all associated areas within the OT. Throughout the research into surgery the researcher was accepted by virtually all the personnel involved in surgery at General Hospital as having a legitimate reason for visiting these spaces, which are off-limits to unauthorized personnel. This degree of access was largely as a consequence of a serendipitous meeting some months previous to the study with a consultant anaesthetist, Dr J., who became a key informant in this study. This chance contact with Dr J. had ended with an invitation to the researcher to discuss the role of anaesthetics in surgery and this led to a series of interviews in which Dr J. expressed great interest in the study. Contact with a wide range of his colleagues in the departments of anaesthetics and surgery at General Hospital followed. In the beginning he smoothed the way for access to the OTs and indeed encouraged as wide an experience of surgery at General Hospital as possible. Later he suggested many personnel who should be interviewed, and using his name these were obtained with no difficulty. Eventually, these new contacts in turn led to personnel without the direct influence of Dr J., and indeed I was concerned not to be too dependent on one informant in the later stages of the study. Looking back on the relationship it is clear that rapport was achieved as a consequence of a shared interest in observation; anaesthetists spend much of their time observing patients and their responses during surgery, and consequently observing surgeons and other personnel in the OT. (This point is taken up much more fully in Chapter 3.) Two other anaesthetists became informants in due course. The only thing I was really able to offer in return for the information and the access was to be someone intelligent to talk to during the periods of tedium during operations when, if the patient is fit, anaesthetists have little or nothing to do apart from occasionally note a reading.

Being the guest of an anaesthetist in the OT has one big advantage: as such, one is relatively free to stand to one side, walk around the theatre and talk to whoever one wishes, or even leave theatre to visit other parts of the surgical complex. On the occasions when my entry to the OT was via a surgeon I was continually being forced to watch the details of surgical technique, even on a few occasions being made to assist the surgeon, duties which (although fascinating) reduced my opportunities to observe the rest of what was going on in the OT.

I must speak briefly about the emotional impact of doing this observation. Before I began the ethnography I has some anxieties about the reality of blood and the unpleasant side of opening bodies and resecting organs. Although as a one-time medical student I had dissected bodies, I was not certain what would be my physical response to seeing surgery. As it happened, I think that I probably experienced the same distancing that other surgical personnel find. This is partly to do with the need to get on with the job, and in my case to keep out of the way and try to observe something, and partly because the techniques of covering all of a body apart from the immediate operation site, removed all sense that there was a person under all the green cloth, undergoing the insult of scalpel or diathermy. Only when the towels were removed at the end of the operation was the identity restored, and by this time the worst was over. I am sure that this distancing contributes to the cavalier way patients are sometimes treated or talked about when on the operating table.

Occasionally, my personal response was more extreme. One operation I saw entailed neurosurgery on a boy of eight, who was in great pain and distress when he was brought to theatre. This episode upset me a great deal, and I found it hard to write about afterwards. It was my impression that some of the staff were also disturbed by this patient, who did not behave with the stoicism that is perhaps expected of patients who are attending for surgery. My response in this case made me think about the material which I was studying in a new light, and perhaps helped me to sustain myself as an outsider, avoiding the tendency when one immerses oneself in a field to go native: in this context, of adopting the generally dispassionate responses to the really rather horrible business of surgery which characterize those I was studying.

An outline of the ethnography

In reporting the data gathered during the ethnography of surgery I shall be guided by my objective of demonstrating how different aspects of the everyday life of surgery constitutes the power of the specialty and its practitioners. Writing ethnography entails methodologies of selecting data so as to constitute something more than merely 'description'. As Hammersley (1990) points out, the claim to provide description which provides valid explanation is one traditionally seen as fraught with problems concerning the author's perspective. As mentioned earlier, the postmodern sociologist is open about her/his values, so perhaps this issue is resolved once one accepts there is no one truth. All I can provide is 'a' social meaning of surgery ultimately. For more discussion of these issues, see Atkinson (1990) and Tyler (1986). The way I have approached the analysis, using a deconstructive strategy, focuses the attention upon places within the discursive activities which constitute the everyday enterprise of surgery, where the discourse seems in some way or other to be problematic. It could be that there are contradictory explanations of what is happening, or that what is said is done is not what is observed to be done, or that actors avoid a subject or are dismissive or just silent. In any ethnography a researcher cannot expect to identify all these 'nodes', and no doubt I have only scratched the surface. Where I have identified a 'node' – to take an example, over the use of surgical masks – I have concentrated my enquiries, refined the observations, and perhaps sought out data outside the ethnographic field. By such strategy, it could be said that I make silences speak, make what has to be obscure, a 'gap', visible. In this way the ideological commitments of discourse, which can work only so long as they are invisible, are made clear. This deconstructive work is hard to describe in the abstract, but it will become clear as the book proceeds. The hardest work is in the detailed gathering of the ethnographic data – the report, I hope, will be straightforward.

In Chapter 2 – entitled 'The Circuits of Hygiene' – the reader is introduced to the field in which surgery occurs, the operating theatre and its immediate environs. I describe in detail the stages of induction, resection and recovery undergone by patients during surgery, and the articulation of these stages with procedures concerned with hygiene, entailing the movements of staff, patients and instruments in ordered circuits in space and time. The chapter considers whether these techniques, basic to the practice of surgery, possess 'rhetorical' attributes which serve to mark out the processes by which surgical healing is claimed to have been achieved, and in the process demarcate hierarchical relations within the surgical team.

In Chapter 3 the fascinating relationship between surgeon and anaesthetist is the focus. Using ethnography and interviews I demonstrate how these two professional groupings rely on each other for much of their work, yet their interests are directly in conflict. The discourses of surgeon and anaesthetist are complementary, and collude in a complex master-discourse on surgical success.

In Chapter 4, the ethnography moves out of the operating theatre, on to the surgical ward. Here the discourses of the surgeon on patients, and in particular on their position in the process of surgical healing is examined. Physiology, wound condition and discharge from hospital provide three themes in this discourse, each intended to demonstrate the power of the surgeon to define patients as healed.

Chapter 5 turns to issues concerning the management of surgery on a daily basis. As will be seen, a surgical list appears to be a highly unmanageable enterprise, and the daily disruption of the smooth running of the operating theatre is the starting point for a deconstruction of the relations between surgeons and managers. The paradox of the clinician who is a manager is used as a pivot for discourse analysis.

The ethnography moves in Chapter 6 to a consideration of day case surgery (DCS) – a case study which illumines themes which have been identified in the previous chapters. The model of surgical healing supplied by DCS turns out to be seriously flawed as a vehicle for the surgical discourse on healing. The implications for the take up of this particular model of doing surgery are significant, and the case illustrates the value of the deconstructive methodology as a means of evaluating medical technologies. Chapter 7 draws together the ethnographic findings to offer an explanation of surgical power grounded in the daily activities of the specialty, which constitute the social meaning of surgery.

2

THE CIRCUITS OF HYGIENE

Introduction

The operating theatre is known to most people through images which have permeated the popular media. Surgeons seem willing to allow television crews to enter their theatres on the least pretext of some new breakthrough. Few operating theatres are now built to incorporate the viewing galleries which provided their name, and the opportunities for those not directly involved in surgical operations to witness precisely what occurs in these spaces has consequently diminished. The operating theatre is one of the most inaccessible 'back-spaces' of the modern hospital, often signposted in code further to reduce the possibility of the casual unwelcome visitor. But it is also at the centre of the surgical enterprise, and it must therefore also be at the centre of this ethnography of surgery. For both these reasons (and I commend this section even to readers who regularly inhabit these spaces – we are often blind to much in the settings we routinely live within), I begin the ethnography in this chapter with a detailed background to life in the operating theatre. Initially I focus on the personnel found in and around the surgical space, and move on to describe the physical layouts of these spaces: the operating theatre suites (abbreviated throughout this book as OT) at General Hospital. It is a report based on my final understanding, gleaned after a prolonged period of fieldwork, even though such basics were a primary concern when I began research in the OT.

Sociologists have recognized how spaces affect interactions, already I have used Goffman's (1959, 1961) notions of front- and back-space. Responding to new interest in the human body as the focus of power, Giddens has recognized (1985) physical space as a limiting factor in agency, as from a different perspective has B. Turner (1986). Medical examples of the effects of spaces on discourse have been documented by Rawlings (1985), Rosengren and DeVault (1963) and Prior

(1988). In some of these discussions there is a tendency towards determinism; architecture is either something which requires certain interactions to occur: this position is clearly counter-factual and may quickly be discarded, or it provides 'cues' which, literally 'built-in' to the fabric of the space as a consequence of historical discourses on sterility or observation for example, provide agents with information which assists them to carry out their interactions correctly or successfully. I wish to take a weaker position: that in certain circumstances architecture makes available to actors a skein of rhetorical devices by which they can support their discursive activities. What I mean by this is that actors – for example surgeons – may draw on the physical arrangements of surgical spaces (among many other resources available) in order to sustain and promote a particular interpretation of what is happening in the OT, an interpretation which is potentially open to challenge from alternative or contradictory analyses by others, perhaps even using other aspects of the architecture so to do.

The clearest example of this concerns sterile procedure, and the second part of this chapter takes this crucial aspect of the surgery – aseptic technique – and examines precisely how it is sustained. My analysis is intended to demonstrate how physical boundaries and barriers enable, and help to constitute, rhetorical figurations which organize sets of movements through the surgical spaces: movements of bodies, staff and instruments. These movements are designated *circuits of hygiene*, acknowledging the etymological root of the word 'hygiene' as a system of rules for promoting health (*OED* s.v. 'hygiene'). Following the 'weak' position outlined above, I would suggest that these circuits are 'sufficient', yet not 'necessary'. Rules *can* be broken, and indeed the variability in OT layout indicates that architecture is no more than an adjunct, a resource to bolster understandings of what should happen in the OT.

This argument is clearest with regard to rules of clothing in the OT. Drawing on the ethnographic data, and interviews with OT staff, I show how rules concerning sterile garb are broken with some impunity and regularity by senior doctors. From this I point to the *rhetorical* nature of these activities, which inscribe into discourse a particular set of social relations between patients, surgeons and other staff. While I thus oppose any analysis of aseptic technique grounded in notions of 'ritual', and therefore distance this analysis from the work of Katz (1984), it is worth noting correspondence between the data gathered at General and hers, gathered in North America. The discussion provides the first opportunity for the methodology of deconstruction to be utilized in this study, in examining observed anomalies concerning the use of surgical masks. This analysis indicates how surgical procedures such as mask-wearing are not only instrumental, but constitutive of, and a consequence of social relations. By examining in great detail the discourses around mask-wearing, one may deconstruct these anomalies to understand how such activities confer and confirm participants' power.

The three 'circuits of hygiene', of patients, of the staff and of the instruments are thus intimately concerned with the first of the 'distinctive' characteristics of surgery – asepsis. But of course they are also concerned with a second – resection, the process by which a patient is physically subject to the surgical intervention, be it removal or repair of a tissue, and with or without involving incision and subsequent closure of a wound. A further opportunity for deconstruction occurs in the final section of this chapter, which describes a 'typical' operation, in terms of the stages of a patient's progression from ward to operating table and back to ward. This detailed description considers how the 'beginning, middle and end' of the operation once again supplies rhetorical information which can assist discourse on the process of surgical healing, and the rights of legitimacy which surgeons possess to undertake such interventions into other people's bodies. The contribution of the third distinctive element – anaesthesia – to these rhetorical figurations will be the subject of Chapter 3.

Operating theatre personnel

Responsibility for an OT on a minute-to-minute basis is held by the theatre sister (charge nurse), who reports to the Operating Department Manager. The theatre sister is responsible for safety, availability of equipment, stocks of drugs and instruments, for ensuring rules of sterility are not broken. Guests in theatre are notified to sister, and if this is not done prior to a theatre session will be quizzed about their identity. On one occasion, on being asked who I was by theatre sister A., and having said that both Mr C. (neurosurgeon) and Dr A. (anaesthetist) had given permission for me to attend, I was told that I should also have asked her: 'I need to know who is here.' She subsequently asserted her authority by telling me where to stand. During a procedure to fit a reservoir to drain cerebrospinal fluid from the ventricle of the brain of a patient, she supplied me with background material in the form of a leaflet about the reservoir.

In theory, a twin theatre suite is staffed with seven trained nursing staff. In each theatre there will be one scrub nurse, one circulating nurse, and an anaesthetic nurse (usually a State Enrolled Nurse (SEN) rather than the more highly qualified State Registered Nurse (SRN)). The seventh nurse will control the flow of lists in the OT.

2.1

OPERATING DEPARTMENT MANAGER NURSE F.: More often there will be six, or sometimes five. We are not happy when there are only five because that relies on two students and occasionally a post-basic nurse on a theatre course.

The anaesthetic nurse, who also helps prepare patients, positioning them or, for example, putting on tourniquets, has taken over many duties previously carried out by an Operating Department Assistant (ODA), although two still remain at General Hospital, one in plastic theatres, the other in thoracic OT. The reason for this replacement, according to one of these two ('John'), was savings on overtime payment.

In almost all the operations observed at General Hospital, elective surgery was conducted by a consultant surgeon. Occasionally, a senior registrar in surgery will be the most senior surgeon present, with access to a consultant for advice if needed. The only times during the fieldwork that an entire list was taken by a non-consultant was in orthopaedic surgery, when a consultant surgeon operated in one theatre, while in the twin theatre Mr K., a 'clinical assistant' (a permanent post just below consultant rank), operated, and would call on his consultant colleague for advice before commencing certain procedures.

The senior surgeon is assisted by a more junior doctor, who will usually stand facing the former across the patient. There is a large degree of hands-on learning done by inexperienced registrars and house doctors, by which they obtain experience of operative techniques. Almost all doctors in a surgical firm (team led by a consultant) senior to house doctors will be intending to pursue a surgical career, or one in which fellowship of a surgical college will be a valuable asset to possess. The techniques which a surgeon will be able to perform are very slowly acquired during the junior (non-consultant) years.

2.2
In a gynaecology theatre, a registrar was being supervised on her first hysterectomy. Although she had previously assisted at many such operations, she was extremely nervous, and was tentative in her cutting. The consequence appeared bizarre to the researcher in that she used the tip of a scalpel gently to incise the uterus as if to mark out a dotted line she could then follow, while asking the consultant if this was the correct line to cut along. When assured that it was correct, she completed the resection.

There is a very strict division of labour between surgeons and the other doctors present – anaesthetists (see Chapter 3 for more on this). The patient is anaesthetized by a consultant or senior registrar anaesthetist, and is monitored throughout the operation by this doctor, or by a junior anaesthetist who will call the consultant if any change occurs. Ambulance personnel on training courses in anaesthesia will sometimes assist a consultant anaesthetist, and on occasions it was observed that such a person was left to monitor a patient under general anaesthetic for short periods when the anaesthetist was not in the operating theatre.

Medical students are occasional visitors to an OT from the university medical school, either as part of a rotation in surgery or in anaesthetics.

Operating theatre suite layout

At General Hospital, surgery is carried out in ten operating theatres, which are organized into five twin suites. While there are some differences between suite

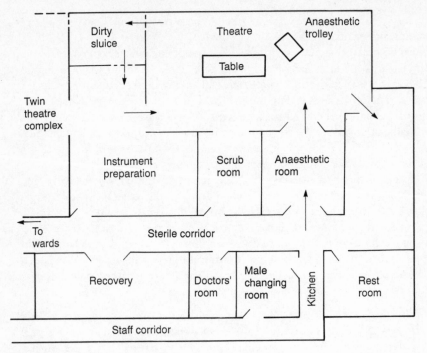

FIGURE 2.1 Floor plan of general surgery theatre.

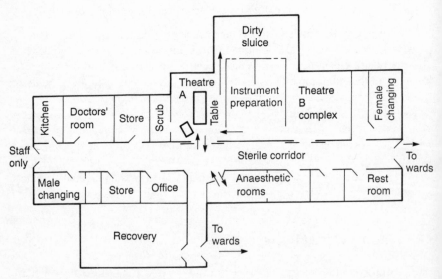

FIGURE 2.2 Floor plan of plastic surgery theatre.

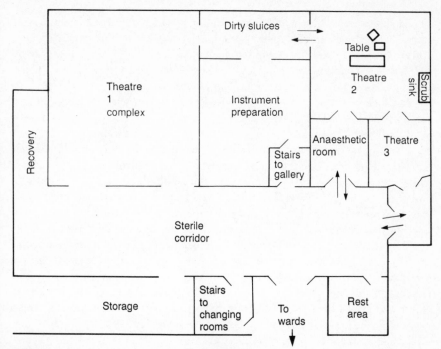

FIGURE 2.3   Floor plan of neuro-surgery theatre.

layout, some features are in common. The two twin general theatre suites, and the twin suite known at the time of field work as Thoracic Theatres, which has now been converted partially for day case surgery, all conform to a similar layout. Figure 2.1, the diagram of one General OT therefore provides a layout for six of the ten theatres at General. Figure 2.2. shows the layout of Plastic Theatres, and Figure 2.3 the layout of Neurosurgery Theatres.

OTs are organized around a central core area, known as the sterile corridor (SC). The entrance(s) to the SC are clearly marked as off-limits to patients, visitors, and staff not authorized to enter, and form the principal barrier and boundary to the OT. Within this barrier a second set of doors marks the boundary beyond which sterile conditions are supposed to apply, and within which precautions are taken to reduce the numbers of infective organisms present. Because floors are disinfected, all categories of personnel (with one exception which I discuss later) passing through the inner doors must first put on plastic overshoes which are available in a box between the two sets of doors. Observations of life within the OT suggest that the institution of the sterile corridor is the principal means of defining the surgical space as separate from the rest of the hospital in terms of hygiene. Almost all surgical personnel use a different route of access into the OT. Either within the first set of doors, or via a discreetly marked staff entrance, access is obtained to a staff corridor, which leads to changing rooms. Changing rooms contain washing and toilet facilities, and stocks of sterile clothing. Suitably garbed, personnel are able to enter the sterile corridor via an internal door from the changing rooms. The mode of entry to the OT distinguishes between OT staff and the other category of person entering the area – patients, and their ward nurse companions.

Each theatre within the twin suite possesses its own anaesthetic room and scrub areas, but shares instrument preparation and instrument sterilization facilities. These latter spaces are situated between the two theatres of a suite, and provide a means of access between theatres without passing through the sterile corridor. This area, consisting of theatres and instrument preparation areas, along with scrub areas, form an inner sanctum within the OT, to which access is limited to specific personnel. The sluice area is accessible from theatre either via a hatchway through which trolleys of instruments can be passed, or a corridor. Instruments are cleaned and sterilized in this area, which is separated from an instrument preparation area normally by a hatchway. The complex separations of dirty and clean personnel noted by Rawlings (1985) in her interesting investigation of this aspect of the circuits of hygiene were not a feature at General Hospital. Scrub areas contain washing facilities and stocks of sterile gowns, gloves and masks for use by surgeons and scrub nurses. Access to scrub areas varies from theatre to theatre as can be seen from Figures 2.1–2.3.

The other areas comprise a recovery room for post-operative patients, and areas for use by staff – offices for doctors and the theatre sister, a rest room, and equipment stock rooms. The OT is thus virtually autonomous of the hospital, and in some OTs such as neurosurgery where all-day lists are conducted, arrangements are made to provide snack luncheon for staff obviating the need to leave the OT between 9 a.m. and late afternoon. Telephones situated in the sterile corridor and in the offices, and the bleep system enable contact with the outside world to be maintained, although it can effectively be kept at a distance by claiming pressure of urgent work to be done in the OT. Informants told the researcher that one of the pleasures of working in surgery was the inaccessibility. The effect which a sterile corridor has on separating the OT from the outside was noted by informants:

2.3

INFECTION CONTROL NURSE: Danger of infection will be used as the excuse for all the expense (of architectural arrangement), but these precautions are also very effective in keeping unwanted people out of theatre.

Within the operating theatre, the operating table is centrally placed. A movable anaesthetics trolley is situated to one end, and is connected to various pipes providing oxygen and anaesthetic gases. The orientation of the patient is therefore limited by the need for anaesthetic access, and the surgical and anaesthetic areas of the theatre are mutually exclusive, as will be seen in greater detail in Chapter 3.

Sterile procedures in surgery

Surgery is an enterprise within health care peculiarly enclosed by 'rules' of conduct. A large proportion of these rules concern the sterility of the OT – the prevention of entry by infective agencies into certain areas whereby infection of surgical wounds, or cross-contamination between patients might result. The more obvious aspects of sterile procedure, for instance the wearing of sterile clothing is complemented by more subtle procedures concerned with the movement of persons and objects within the OT. I will first consider sterile garb, and then move on to these 'circuits of hygiene'.

All personnel who enter the operating theatre wear a mask, clogs or boots, and a J-cloth cap – or for some surgeons, a hood. At General, supplies of these are provided in the changing rooms. Male personnel wear a linen shirt and trousers (greens), while female theatre personnel wear a white dress. This gender difference in garb leads to some status problems; because female doctors have to change in the women's changing room, in most OTs they have access only to a uniform which is traditionally equated with (lower status) nursing staff. In the neurosurgery OT however, the sterile clothing stocks are held in a cupboard between the separate male and female changing rooms.

2.4
Two female anaesthetics registrars who were assisting Dr A. came to neurosurgery theatre dressed in 'greens', the pyjama tops and trousers worn by male doctors at General, but by all clinical staff at some other hospitals. However, a female guest, a young researcher, was given a white dress to wear while visiting the OT, and was hence equated with nursing as opposed to clinical staff.

Aspects of garb, and the rhetoric that the change from street clothes to greens supplies, are considered in detail later in this chapter. Surgeons, assistants and a scrub nurse, that is, all personnel who will have contact with the 'sterile field' – the area of wound and surrounding towels – wear a sterile gown, gloves, and scrub their hands and forearms prior to an operation. The scrub is a highly routinized procedure, taught to neophytes and conducted in an area normally separated from the operating room, although in neurosurgical OT it consists merely of a scrub sink in one corner of the theatre. The person scrubbing spends an allotted period washing the hands and forearms in antiseptic soap and scrubbing the nail-bed. The hands are then dried. A sterile gown is then taken from a shelf, and put on. This requires the assistance of another person, usually a nurse or visitor, who will tie the gown at the back. Sterile gloves are then removed from a pack and put on. This has to be done without touching the outside of the glove with the hand, although the hand has been scrubbed. On one occasion I was invited to scrub, so that I could get very close to the sterile field to observe the operation, and found the procedure very difficult, to the amusement of the nurse who was demonstrating the techniques and ensuring that sterility was not compromised by a neophyte.

The cooperative effort involving in sterile garbing breaks across status boundaries to an extent, and is another example of the 'separateness' of the OT. Part of the research bargain came to be the use of the researcher to assist sterile personnel tying and untying gowns, moving non-sterile equipment, and carrying the fibre-optic cord attached to one surgeon's head-lamp, in procession around the theatre. The researcher was used to make up for shortage of nursing support needed to protect sterility. However there are limits to this cooperative effort, defined by tradition:

2.5
SURGEON MR T.: There was a time when you could demand a particular
    instrument. Now you take what you are given.

and by status:

2.6
A junior (non-consultant) surgeon was operating in plastic theatre. He
asked for some service or other from a nurse. She performed this adding in
a sarcastic tone of voice: 'Would sir like me to mop his sweating brow?'

Once the surgeon or scrub nurse is garbed in sterile gown and gloves, s/he must not touch anything unsterile, including mask or cap. So these have to be in place before scrubbing, and must remain untouched throughout the operation. Some surgeons change masks between operations, others wear the same mask throughout a list. Masking is an area of sterile procedure where rules of method have a degree of latitude, as will be seen later.

The scrub nurse and assisting surgeon prepare the anaesthetized patient. The wound area is disinfected with an iodine paint. In some surgery, a sterile plastic skin is now stuck over the wound area to prevent possibility of bacteria from the skin adjacent to the wound entering the incision. Towels are spread over the patient, leaving a small rectangular area for operating within. When the head is not involved, it, and the anaesthetic equipment is separated from the operating site by a curtain of sterile towelling. In neuro-surgery, the face of the patient is covered as is the rest of her/his body with towelling, leaving only the cranium exposed.

Towelling an operation is part of the rhetoric of the OT as well as being instrumental. Towelling creates a sterile barrier: beneath a towel is a non-sterile area, which is accessible only to non-sterile personnel. Any piece of equipment which is to be above the operation, for example an X-ray gun in orthopaedic surgery, or a microscope for plastic surgery, is covered either with towels or in sterile plastic sheeting. This separation of the sterile from the non-sterile has some odd consequences when what is under the towel is the patient;

2.7
A monitoring device attached to the hand of a patient undergoing major

vascular surgery had become inoperative. The anaesthetist had to burrow under the towelling, along the side of the naked patient, to re-attach the device. When this was achieved, he asked the assisting surgeon not to lean against the towelling covering the patient's arm, to avoid disconnection a second time.

Instruments are brought from the instrument preparation room laid out on towel-covered trolleys. These are positioned such that they can be accessed by the scrub nurse, often on gantries over the recumbent patient. Unscrubbed nurses will open packages containing sterile contents such as disposable syringes, swabs and any prosthetic devices to be used. The outside of these packages are non-sterile, so they are designed so that the sterile contents will drop out on to the sterile surface, where they can be accessed by the scrub nurse. The scrub nurse passes sterile instruments to the surgeon with the right hand, and takes them from him/her with the left. No other personnel may come into contact with sterile instruments or towels, or sterile personnel. On one occasion when I became participant as well as observer, an extra pair of hands was required to retract the skin layer of a particularly obese patient during an operation, in order to gain satisfactory wound access. This task required considerable strength, so because of his gender, and a shortage of nursing staff, I was asked to assist by holding the skin retractor. However, because I was not scrubbed, I could not touch the retractor, and there was no time for me to scrub. So a piece of sterile bandage was tied to the eyelet of the retractor (which is shaped like a pair of scissors) and I was given the other end of this bandage to pull. A subtle means of breaching, yet technically sustaining, the sterile/non-sterile distinction was thereby devised.

Some instruments will be used more than once during an operation, but any instruments which are deemed to have lost their sterility, by contact with the skin, or with gastro-intestinal contents, will be discarded. Discarded instruments are removed by unscrubbed personnel. The circuit of hygiene associated with instruments is considered further below.

The anomaly of the surgical mask

Within the OT, masks are worn only in the operating theatre, in the instrument preparation room, and on some occasions in the anaesthetic room. In the anaesthetic room, masks are not normally worn, nor do anaesthetic personnel wear sterile gowns or gloves. The exception is if a spinal or epidural anaesthetic is to be given, when the anaesthetist will wash (but not scrub) his/her hands, put on sterile gloves, gown and mask. These procedures are considered as sorts of mini-operations carried out by an anaesthetist, and so warrant the mask and gloves. Other personnel in the anaesthetic room also wear their masks during these procedures.

Wearing a mask marks a boundary around the core area of the OT in terms of sterility (see Figure 2.1). In the anaesthetic room, masks worn by anaesthetist and anaesthetic nurse are normally pulled down, to dangle around the chin. (The 'rest' position, which all unscrubbed theatre personnel will adopt throughout the OT, in the rest room, office, and if called away, elsewhere in the hospital.) The patient having been induced into unconsciousness, before opening the theatre doors to wheel the trolley bearing the patient into theatre, anaesthetist and nurse will first pull up their masks. One might therefore assume that the rule is that an operating theatre is an area in which masking is essential in order to prevent infective agents entering theatre from the respiratory tracts of staff. However, this is not so when a patient has been treated; i.e. once an operation is complete and the skin incision is sewn.

2.8
A surgeon, Mr M., completed an abdominal operation, and having sutured the muscle layer, left his assistant to close the skin. He de-gowned, and having discarded used gloves and masks returned to watch the final stages of the suturing and dressing, standing quite close to the prostrate patient.

2.9
Anaesthetic nurse J. was clearing up after an operation, and prior to the next patient's arrival in theatre, and was talking to the researcher, who was masked. She had her mask dangling below her chin.

So when a theatre does not contain a patient, or the patient has undergone surgery, masking is not necessary. Even when a patient is undergoing surgery, certain personnel may remove their masks.

2.10
The researcher asked Dr A., the anaesthetist in neuro-surgical OT, if he always had assistance. He said that often he did not, and he would bring his coffee into theatre (necessitating removal of mask).

2.11
An ambulance-man trainee went for a coffee break during an operation. He brought Dr B. (anaesthetist) and the researcher cups of coffee in theatre. Dr B. said to the researcher: 'You had better take yours outside. It is only consultants who are allowed to drink their coffee here.'

Even the method of mask-wearing varied. When the mask is in its operational position, is is intended to cover both nose and mouth, and secured above and below with tapes. In this way, it is close fitting below the chin; any explosive emission of droplets will be directed sideways away from the operation wound. Surgeons are taught not to turn their heads to sneeze – this will have the effect of directing the emission into the wound. However, the researcher observed most anaesthetists and many surgeons wearing a mask such as only to cover the mouth. One anaesthetist wore his with only top tapes tied, so that the mask hung loose, with its lower tapes dangling. Getting informants to talk about these observations was interesting. How a mask is worn depends on comfort:

2.12

DR M., OBSTETRIC ANAESTHETIST AND OPERATING DEPARTMENT MANAGER: There is a battle between bacteriological sterility and workability. You are supposed to wear a mask like this [*demonstrates*], but many wear it like this [*under the nose*] claiming that their spectacles are misted up if they wear it over the nose.

Convention also is a factor. At Southern, the obstetric unit had decided that masks were no longer to be worn during delivery.

2.13

DR M.: Childbirth is natural, so there was pressure to make it so – and that means not wearing surgical masks. Access to theatre is limited to people who are properly dressed, but we found that new mothers in recovery were neglected as a result, so we made access to recovery rooms open.

There is also debate over the value of masks. I devoted some time trying to generate discourse on masking after observing the variety of methods and extent of usage of masks at General.

2.14

THEATRE SISTER: These things work for two minutes, and then have no effect. At the Children's Hospital they've stopped wearing them. There's no evidence that they work.
RESEARCHER: So it's traditional, and symbolic?
THEATRE SISTER: Yes. You do what the boss says, so here we do some things which are not done elsewhere.

2.15

NURSE MANAGER F.: Filter masks work better now than they did – the best ones last two to three hours.

2.16

INFECTION CONTROL NURSE B.: Discarding masks might have little effect so long as little speaking occurred around the patient, this having some effect on air movement.

2.17

THEATRE SISTER NURSE G.: Antibiotics are doing the job at the moment. you could do an operation in the middle of a cornfield and be as safe. Here the air conditioning doesn't work. And it's a problem with all the comings and goings. In plastic theatre, you can have sales reps in their street clothes standing at the door of the theatre chatting to the surgeon during an operation. There's a hospital in ——— where they lock the doors and bring the telephone in at the beginning of an operation. You might think that's a lot of trouble, but you'd feel happy having an operation there. In Australia, the antibiotics no longer work.

The discontinuity between the received knowledge of sterile practice and the actual activities which seem to compromise these practices was an issue which, despite being raised regularly by me, never achieved what I considered to be satisfactory resolution. Informants were unable to provide any rationale for their behaviour. If I suggested that personnel 'liked' to wear the mask, that it 'meant more' than being simply a scientifically valid practice, this met with strong denial or incredulity and threatened the continuity of the research bargain with some informants. What can be made of this recalcitrant datum? Perhaps it may be possible to shed some light on the discontinuity by looking at *who* disregards sterile practice.

Nurses speak of surgeons as seeing themselves as 'above infection'. An infection control nurse commented: 'You very seldom find both surgeon and anaesthetist with masks adjusted properly.' Student nurses, on the other hand look as if they practice in front of the mirror, so perfectly straight are their masks. Nurses are taught to wear them whenever in theatre, although attachment to anaesthetists, as noted above, seems to contaminate this perfection. So perhaps it is simply an issue of status, and the degree of compliance with masking routine is inversely related to the position in the hierarchy of the OT. As has been seen in the above extracts, nurses are aware of the doubtful value of masks, yet it is the doctors who flout the rules, yet are silent over this matter.

2.18
DR M.: Nurses are very conservative and fairly rigid in their outlook. They
    are by far the best people for maintaining surgical sterility.

This suggests that doctors need not concern themselves with what is a matter beyond their control, nothing to do with their skills and flexibility. This seems the point at which a deconstruction can begin to make the silence speak.

Deconstructing the surgical mask

As this is the first deconstructive exercise in this book, it is worth briefly explaining how it is achieved. It has become trendy in some texts to talk of 'deconstruction' to mean any process which claims to find the 'hidden' meaning of a piece of discourse, and often it is unclear how this is done. I use the term very explicitly, following Derrida (1978). A helpful definition is provided by Culler (1983, p. 86):

... to deconstruct a discourse is to show how it undermines the philosophy it asserts, the hierarchical opposition on which it relies, by identifying in the text the rhetorical oppositions that produce the supposed ground of argument, the key concept or premise.

and this position is expanded in Flax's (1990, pp. 37–38) description:

> Deconstructive readers are disrespectful to authority, attentive to suppressed tensions or conflicts within the text, and suspicious of all 'natural' categories, essentialist oppositions and representational claims. . . . In a deconstructive reading one looks for what has been suppressed within the text. . . . Given the premise that the Real is always heterogeneous and differentiated, it follows that whenever a story appears unified or whole, something must have been suppressed in order to sustain the appearance of unity. . . . Recovering the suppressed allows the strains and self-divisions that are an at least equally important part of the story to reappear. The deconstructionist is particularly interested in the strategies a work uses to claim its representational authority . . .

The first step must be the closest possible reading of the discursive material. As an aid to analysis, in deconstruction the structuralist notion of binary oppositions is adapted to demonstrate how discourses are constructed. The steps can be summarized as follows:

1 *Position*: One pole of an opposition has been privileged, but in fact this pole relies upon negation.
2 *Negation*: The opposing pole, which is in fact the more important in defining the opposition.
3 *Negation of negation*: This second pole is obscured or denied in discourse in order to make the ideology work.
4 *Deconstruction*: The operation of the discourse is demonstrated by exposing the negated pole.

This deconstruction exposes how discourse has sought to impose a position over other possible definitions. Once exposed, spaces can be opened up which can offer different and perhaps more varied ideas. In examining ethnographic data of course one is not dealing with a 'text', but with an open-ended set of practices, to which more are continually being added. Ethnography can take a snapshot of these practices but not supply a definitive account. So all that can be done in analysis is to identify particular points at which discourse seems to be at its most slippery, where different actors supply different accounts, where contradictions are seen to be glossed or obscured, where there are strains and divisions (to use Flax's terms), or where actors lay claim to particular authority to support their discourses. For these reasons, when I speak of 'deconstructing' or 'deconstruction', I would ask the reader to accept the positions developed as suggestive, evocative, rather than final.

With discontinuity and contradiction as the starting point for deconstruction, what can be made of the ethnographic data concerning the anomalies of masking reported above? It seems to me that the data indicates a polarity between the mask as instrumental on one hand and the mask as signifier or marker on the other: that is, between the mask's claimed function as a hygienic barrier, and its ability to demarcate its wearer as someone who is engaged in the business of surgery. The deconstruction looks as follows:

Position: Instrumentality of sterile mask.

Negation: Mask as social marker of legitimacy of activity, that one is doing 'surgery' rather than butchery or assault.

Negation of negation: Masking is claimed simply as a 'rational' activity, denying any significance for the mask as a signifier of the right to do 'surgery', even though without this signification of the right, the instrumentality of the mask would be irrelevant, a grotesque adjunct to some bizarre violence on another person.

Deconstruction: Surgical discourse uses the mask as a marker of rights, while claiming it is 'just' a technical procedure. The surgical mask is a rhetorical device which simply marks out what is being done as legitimate activity, and the right of the wearer to be involved in the enterprise. The mask stands for the legitimacy of the technique of surgery – it is metonymic for it.

This perspective on the mask is developed much more fully in a study of the historical preference for asepsis with its rhetorical garbs and discourse on purity, over antisepsis with its rival discourse of bacteriological 'cleanliness' (Fox, 1988). However, in the context of the present, there is a problem. As has been seen, there is now serious doubt over the value of the mask as an instrumental technique. Clinicians, as highly educated professionals, could be mocked if they were seen to be continuing to unquestioningly use the mask as hygienic barrier, perhaps at the expense of other aspects of hygiene. Under these circumstances the authority of the surgeon to do surgery could be seriously undermined. Deconstruction offers a new reading of the data in this situation.

Position: The mask is of doubtful instrumental efficacy.

Negation: The mask is still a valuable indicator that one is doing 'surgery'.

Negation of negation: High status staff (clinicians) wear the mask 'rhetorically', indicating that they are hedging their bets on the value of the barrier. Other (low status) staff are expected to wear the mask religiously, thus marking them as the irrational acceptors of received wisdom, without the ability to judge academic research in bacteriology.

Deconstruction: Senior staff in the OT are torn between scientific understanding and the distinctiveness derived from the mask. They mark their ability to 'rise above hygiene' by cursory or idiosyncratic wearing of the mask. There is a secondary gain, as it enables a further marking of their status in the proceedings as the principal actors in the drama of surgical healing.

This reading offers new readings of much of the earlier material on hygienic practices. However, the use of hygiene as a rhetoric which enhances status is a position which was not immediately clear prior to deconstruction. As will be seen throughout this book, similar examples continue to appear. Before turning to analysis of the movements of patients, instruments and staff through the OT, for the sake of completeness, and to supply further support for the previous deconstruction, I will look briefly at a corollary of hygienic technique, the discourse on contamination.

Contamination

While most sterile practices are intended to protect the patient from the surgical environment (including personnel), from time to time mention was made by informants, usually only in response to specific questioning, of the role of surgical garb as protection against contamination.

2.19

OPERATING DEPARTMENT MANAGER NURSE F.: Theatre nurses are at risk more than their colleagues on the ward because of the risk of inoculation of body fluids – it's always possible that a patient with HIV or hepatitis will come in. Staff need to be convinced that the precautions are as foolproof as we can make them, but there is always a risk.

Theatre nurses receive globulin vaccination against serum hepatitis because of the high risk of exposure to body fluids, while, as Nurse F. continued: 'With the orderlies and junior nursing staff there is a need for psychological counselling to cope with the risk.' This suggestion that 'professionalism' entered into acceptance of contamination risks was echoed by a surgeon in plastic theatre, when a patient with many tattoos was being prepared:

2.20

SURGEON MR T.: Never a month goes by that we don't nick ourselves with a scalpel or other instrument, and I suppose we should be concerned about the risk, but we don't generally do anything.

RESEARCHER: I suppose the gloves offer some protection?

MR T.: Yes, once a week I tear a glove, so they may help.

RESEARCHER: Do you take precautions when you have a patient who might be a risk?

MR T.: Well, it's only if there is inoculation with blood that it's a problem.

RESEARCHER: What about blood spray into the eyes?

MR T.: That can be a danger I suppose. I often wear lenses [binocular magnification attachment], so they have a double use.

When a patient who was having needle marks removed from her arm was being treated, surgeons and scrub nurses wore visors against the spray of blood (the operative technique was to remove the topmost layer of skin with a drill fitted with an abrasive wheel). No other precautions were taken, but Dr J. (the anaesthetist) told the researcher (very obliquely) that the patient could be high risk for hepatitis or HIV, and the eye-protecting precautions, while arousing hilarity among the theatre personnel, would have been understood as a warning to take extra care. (The risks of HIV infection from blood during surgery were slowly being recognized in the surgical community at the time of this fieldwork, and it is probable that much more care is now taken.)

As in the previous analysis, distinction is made by these informants between the high status staff, for whom professionalism is translated into a discourse on the need to accept some risk in order to perform their healing role appropriately, as compared to low-grade staff who are not expected (in this discourse) to have these professional commitments. There is not really enough data here for a formal deconstruction, but the analogies with the previous discussion of the use of masks are suggestive that here, too, instrumental procedures are used as adjuncts in the discourse on status differences within the surgical staff. Before turning to the significance of hygienic practice for the movements which characterize surgery (the circuits of hygiene), I will digress to fill in some detail of the historical innovation of sterile clothing in surgery.

The early history of aseptic clothing

A popular myth is that asepsis was the historical successor to Listerian antisepsis. In fact it was a parallel innovation, and while Lister was battling against resistance to antisepsis, aseptic practices were already being introduced, the earliest innovator being Lister's own junior in Glasgow, William MacEwen. Within years of Lister's first paper on antisepsis, and reputedly to the mockery of colleagues including Lister, MacEwen discarded his frock-coat in favour of a sterilizable white apron (Bowman, 1942, p. 61). Aseptic clothing was innovated unevenly over the four decades following MacEwen's example. In comparison to the opposition which met antiseptic practice and germ theory, this innovation of asepsis seemed to have been non-controversial to the extent that it did not elicit any great discourse in the same medical journals which had been so scathing of Listerism. This silence has the effect of making any real history of asepsis difficult to piece together, and the following short history of aseptic practices produced from those records of aseptic innovation which exist is no doubt far from complete. For a longer discussion, see Fox (1988).

Gloves

Gloves were adopted in the first instance as a means of protection against the irritating antiseptic chemicals used in operations. Halsted is generally regarded as the first, in 1878, to permit the use of gloves in the operating room, not while operating or assisting, but to prevent inflammation of his nurse's hands by the mercuric chloride antiseptic used to sterilize instruments. His successor,

Bloodgood was the first to use them while operating in 1893, at the Johns Hopkins University Hospital (Mitchell, 1945, p. 902; Fisher, 1977, p. 275). A photograph in MacCormack's 1880 *Antiseptic Surgery* shows an operator with bare hands (p. 165). Gloves are not mentioned in Schimmelbusch's text of 1895, according to Gerster's 1888 surgical text hands are to be scrubbed with soap, and then rinsed in antiseptic (p. 19). A column in 1914, in the newly published *British Journal of Surgery*, describing eminent surgeon's techniques, noted that Professor Garre of Bonn wore gloves only in septic cases, although Bland Sutton was noted to wear boiled gloves. An ambiguity surrounding the gloves' use is notable in a surgical text of 1912 (Bidwell, 1912, p. 14):

> When doing any operation, it is certainly advisable to wear rubber gloves, on account of the practical impossibility of completely sterilizing the hands. Again the use of rubber gloves prevents any risk of the surgeon's own hand becoming infected, and so carrying infection to another case.

Subsequently, gloves were to become adopted to protect the patient, rather than the surgeon (Mitchell, 1945, p. 902).

Gowns

It has been noted that MacEwen's white gown was the first aseptic item of dress to be worn during surgery. It was to become popular rapidly with the surgical profession. The German surgeon Von Neuber was probably the first to boil his gown, in 1883 (Fisher, 1977, p. 275). Street clothes were acceptable to MacCormack in 1880, but Gerster (1988, p. 19) advocated aprons eight years later. Lockwood remarked in 1896 (p. 162) that in his operating theatre

> The surgeon and his assistants remove their coats, turn up their shirt sleeves, and put on aprons to protect them from the jets of blood. . . . The apron, having not been sterilized, must never be touched with the disinfected hands.

Surgeons operating in all-encompassing suits 'of some light material' are illustrated in Beck's text of 1895 (facing p. 241). At Bland Sutton's theatre, 'visitors are allowed in the theatre galleries without gown or overshoes, but those privileged to walk about the floor must wear a sterile gown' (*British Journal of Surgery*, 1915a, p. 111). In Vienna also, 'all who take part in the operation wear sterilized gowns' at Von Eisenberg's clinic (*British Journal of Surgery*, 1915b, p. 329).

Masks

The surgical texts are most silent over the innovation of face masks. Perhaps this is appropriate. Indeed at Sir Victor Horsley's operations 'loud talking and coughing were strictly forbidden, great stress being laid on the danger of wound infection by contamination in this way' (*British Journal of Surgery*, 1914a, p. 515). The issue of contamination by breath was clearly debated in surgical circles. Schimmelbusch, in 1895 (p. 11), stated:

> There is among doctors as well as among the laity, a widely prevalent belief that expired air is poisonous, and the fables which formerly endowed monsters with a poisonous breath that destroyed everything that it encountered is a striking example . . . many investigations have been undertaken and these have unanimously resulted in showing that instead of fission fungi being given off from the respiratory tract, they are taken up . . . expired air can only become a vehicle for germs if sputum, mucous secretions, or even particles of tissue are coughed out with them.

Unfortunately these studies are not referenced. Casteneda (1961, p. 423) notes that masks were mentioned in passing by the Polish surgeon Mikuliez-Radecki in 1897. By 1911 masks were being advocated to counteract droplet infection while talking, or in the case of oral sepsis, nasal catarrh or carious teeth (Bidwell, 1912, p. 282). Garre did not wear a face mask 'although operating room techniques are mainly on the orthodox aseptic plan' (*British Journal of Surgery*, 1914b, p. 696). Nor did Bland Sutton use a mask at the Middlesex hospital a year later (*British Journal of Surgery*, 1915a, p. 110), although in the same year it was reported that at Watson Cheyne's clinic (*British Journal of Surgery*, 1915c, p. 325):

> Masks for the nose and mouth are worn by all in the immediate vicinity of the operating table, but long before their introduction into surgery Sir Watson had imposed an 'area of silence' around the patient, and had established a code of grunts by which his needs were communicated to his assistants.

Although masks were universally adopted by the 1920s (Fletcher, 1977, p. 20), controversy continues. Ritter *et al.* (1975, p. 50), concluded that 'masks most definitely altered the projective effect introduced by talking and breathing'. However, other studies indicate masks had no effect on reducing infection during operation wound dressing (Collins and Bibby, 1981, p. 18) or during operations (Mitchell, 1981; Orr, 1981, p. 390–391).

Understanding resection: the circuits of hygiene

So far in this chapter the organization of surgery within the OT has been described by reference to architectural spaces and personnel. But, in addition, the surgical order has been shown to be modulated through certain routines of sterile practice based on the theory of asepsis, the removal of infective agencies from the vicinity of the operation wound. The basics of these practices, sterile garb, scrubbing, form the ground rules, and as has been seen, have some bearing on the social relations of surgery. These basics, however, are only part of the business of asepsis, and I now want to consider how they interact with the architecture of the OT to constitute complex routines concerned with the movement of things and bodies, which I call 'circuits of hygiene'. The rest of this chapter is concerned with examining these circuits, which are extremely important in determining the routine nature of surgery in the modern OT. It is within this context that analysis of the actual business of resection, the opening of a patient and removal or repair of a tissue, will be considered. Resection gains its significance only as part of the movements of bodies through the surgical space, it is one part of a larger process.

While it is necessary to describe these movements, what is of interest here is not the architecture or the movements themselves, but the discourse which the circuits of hygiene make available. I hope to demonstrate how the circuits supply rhetorical markers which indicate that what is being done can be labelled as surgery, as a form of healing.

If this last sentence seems extraordinary, if it seems absurd that one should need such markers, consider the following. What usually happens in elective surgery is that a patient comes with some pathology which needs resolution by resection or repair. This is carried out and then the patient is 'healed'. Has the patient thus changed from a status of 'ill' to one of 'well'? In a few cases, this is a reasonable definition of pre- and post-surgical status, but there would be considerable difficulties associated with such a typification in many cases, where both the subjective experience of the patient and the clinical position would be that strictly speaking s/he is 'iller' after the operation than before: suffering pain and shock from the wound, the after-effects of the anaesthetic, and perhaps emotional distress. In the extreme, the patient may die of her/his surgery.

Any healing technique which makes its patients worse than they were before treatment is likely to face opposition, and no doubt many techniques such as bleeding have fallen by the wayside for this reason. Surgery requires a patient to put great trust in statistics, the likelihood that in the long term the benefits outweigh the short-term discomfort and disability. So we might expect that discourse on surgery has sought ways to resolve or more probably *obscure* the paradox, and indeed it is quite easy to identify some. Notions such as 'five-year survival' following cancer surgery are part of a surgical discourse on recovery which is attempting to grapple with this paradox, which in the extreme claims that 'the operation was a success, but the patient died'.

What I am arguing in this book is that these strategies are intricately tied up with the whole surgical process, and that ethnography can unravel some of them. Because the real paradox is that people submit to the insults of surgery, and that surgery is the highest status medical specialty in the West, apart perhaps now from obstetrics, despite the risks, the failures and the pain.

In the context of the investigation of the routines of the OT, one can thus argue that each circuit of hygiene represents an imperative by which the hygiene of surgery is maintained and promoted. The direction of movement ensures that successful hygiene ensues. 'Hygiene' is used here in a double sense. In the narrower sense, hygiene consists of the science of sanitation, cleanliness and sterility. This may be designated hygiene[1]. However, the emic roots of 'hygiene' are wider: 'hygiene' was the knowledge and practice which concerned itself with the promotion and protection of 'health', deriving from Hygeia, goddess of health and daughter of Aesculapius in Greek mythology (*OED* s.v. 'hygiene'; 'Hygeia'). This is hygiene[2]. This wider notion of hygiene as health is appropriate to the understanding of the procedures conducted in the OT, concerned as they are with the restoration and promotion of health in patients undergoing surgical healing. While the circuits of hygiene pertaining to staff and instruments act to ensure hygiene[1], also they are concerned with hygiene[2]: the transition of the patient from her/his unhealthy status prior to healing to a more healthy status as healed. The patient's own circuit of hygiene, her/his movement through the surgical space to perform this status passage, is concerned foremost with hygiene[2].

In Figure 2.1, arrows indicate the direction in which instruments, staff and patients usually move. There are no rules in the forms of signs or physical impedimentia to govern which directions are permissible, although of course barriers in the form of architectural construction limit possible movements. Yet there clearly appear to be conventions which lay down how staff, patients and instruments may move; it would be considered extremely unusual (and probably dangerous) were a patient or an instrument to move in an unconventional direction. The arbitrariness of some conventions pertaining to staff is more obvious. For example, there appears to be nothing preventing the scrub room being used as a thoroughfare, but it is conventional that surgeons do not use the anaesthetic room as a thoroughfare. Conventions can also be altered:

2.21

SURGEON MR P.: At G. [a new private hospital], when commissioned, a red line on the floor demarcated sterile areas in the OT. However, the inclusion of the coffee-room within this boundary prevented surgeons' colleagues dropping by for coffee, thus disrupting a convention of hospital sociability. The red line was quickly re-painted to exclude the coffee-room from the sterile area.

The physical movements which constitute the circuits of hygiene are of course accompanied by particular activities: the legitimacy of an activity may indeed depend upon where or by whom it is carried out. As noted earlier in this chapter, drinking coffee is illegitimate in theatre, unless the imbiber is a consultant. To separate the different circuits is thus somewhat unnatural, and overlap obviously occurs. Because the principal interest here is with the impact of the circuits upon the patient, and with the phases of resection undergone by the patient, the bulk of the following ethnographic section will be devoted to the patient's passage through the OT. Firstly, however, the circuits pertaining to staff and instruments will be described, where their interaction with the patient is not covered in the main section.

The staff circuit

Personnel working in the OT (surgeons, anaesthetists, theatre and anaesthetic nurses, operating department assistants (ODAs), students and auxiliaries) enter the suite along the staff corridor, the entrance to which is outside the inner doors to the sterile corridor (SC). From the staff corridor they can enter the men's and women's changing rooms, which are equipped with lavatory, washing facilities and shower, and in which are supplies of sterile clothing, shoes, masks and caps. Personnel discard their street clothes, although it seems acceptable to retain socks, underwear and tights. Theatre clothes can be quite revealing, and the whole procedure of changing seems to separate the OT from the outside, with its conventions of modesty. Surgeons who go on to the wards wearing theatre greens take care to fasten the side vent of their trousers which usually reveals bare flesh in theatre. Once changed, staff may enter the sterile area, which includes rest rooms, office, stores and telephone in addition to theatres and associated facilities. The kitchen is an ambiguous area in which sterile personnel prepare coffee, while access is also possible from the (non-sterile) staff corridor for auxiliaries who perform domestic duties.

Ward nurses enter the OT with patients through the main OT doors, having put on overshoes. Porters are exempt from this rule, but they take patients only to the anaesthetic room, and collect them from the recovery area, they do not enter theatre, and rarely pass through the outer doors of the anaesthetic room. By not wearing overshoes, porters no doubt contaminate the SC, but this just seems to be ignored. Ward nurses and porters do not work *in* theatre, and are seen as outsiders. However theatre staff are dependent upon them for providing a flow of patients.

2.22
Surgeons and other staff were ready to start an afternoon list at 2 p.m. A telephone call was made to bring the first patient from the ward. However, it was the ward nurse's lunch break, and a nurse could not be spared to accompany a patient. There was a 20 minute wait until the patient arrived. Dr J. said, 'this happens every day. The ward sister knows we start at 2 p.m., but always sends the shift to lunch then, so we are always delayed.'

At the completion of their duties, staff pass back through changing rooms into the non-sterile world, discarding used greens in laundry baskets in the changing rooms.

The instrument circuit

Some details of the instrument circuit pertaining to sterile procedure have been recorded above. Instruments begin their circuit in the preparation room when they are removed from steam autoclaves. In the autoclave they are sterilized in wire baskets bearing the name of the theatre. For a particular operation there is a designated complement of instruments which will be required, and it is up to the theatre sister to ensure that the correct set are prepared prior to the operation. At General Hospital there is a shortage of instruments, so a list containing a number of similar operations may be delayed while instruments are sterilized between operations.

2.23
A patient with an anal fistula is ready to be operated upon. There is a delay because according to the list the planned procedure was an Investigation under Anaesthetic (IuA), and the surgeon has decided to repair the fistula. The nursing staff complain that they did not know what to prepare for; the surgeons complain as they stand around gowned. The anaesthetist has to connect an ECG to the patient because the anaesthetic is going to last longer than was the case for the relatively minor IuA procedure.

Nursing staff have a responsibility to ensure instruments are of a satisfactory standard. Surgeons can be highly critical:

2.24
SURGEON MRS A. TO CHARGE NURSE: This laparoscopy needle will not work, it doesn't move freely . . . give me another. [*Scrub nurse passes another.*] No, this one is no good either. [*Scrub nurse has to go to preparation room for a third needle.*]
MRS A.: We are not going to start badly this morning, are we?

Instruments are laid out on trays covered with green sterile towels and other equipment such as bowls of water are positioned so the scrub nurse can access instruments as required. Scrub nurses are highly knowledgeable about operating technique, and will have a good idea what instruments will be needed as an operation progresses. They also learn a strict etiquette in relation to passing instruments.

2.25
NURSE C.: X. [a certain surgeon] is always reaching over and taking instruments. I slapped him on the hand. I feel like saying, 'Stop it, that's my domain. But I'll say that I'm learning, and I can't learn if he takes the instruments'.
NURSE D.: We're all learning.

2.26
Nurse C. had pulled out a length of sticking tape during the dressing of a post-operative wound on a hand. The surgeon asked for a bandage instead.
SCRUB NURSE D. TO NURSE C.: 'You shouldn't anticipate in plastic [surgery], it's fatal.'

The scrub nurse uses the right hand for sterile instruments, and takes used instruments in the left hand. They are deposited in a dirty tray, or laid to one side (for example, in the case of the scalpel used to cut the muscle layer, which may be needed further) or in antiseptic if contaminated by body fluid (for example, the instruments inserted in the urethra during a trans-urethric resection of prostrate, TURP). Dirty instruments are dispatched to the sluice for washing and sterilisation via the hatchway in Theatres N, thus following a different route out of theatre than that into theatre of clean instruments. This completes the instrument circuit.

The patient circuit

In the following section I document a 'typical' elective operation. The description coalesces aspects of many such operations observed during the period of fieldwork, and the intention is to provide an overall understanding of the context in which resection takes place. Where variants on the theme are common, these are noted.

A patient due for surgery is brought from his/her ward to the OT by a member of the portering staff. At General this may involve travelling some distance between buildings; the plastic OT is a free-standing block, as are many of the surgical wards. On the ward, the patient has been dressed in an operation gown, and transferred from his/her bed to a trolley, upon which they are transported to the OT. Occasionally, if due for a very minor operation involving local anaesthesia, the patient may be brought to the OT in a wheelchair: this was only observed in plastic OT and endoscopy clinic (a non-sterile theatre attached to thoracic theatres not considered in this work). Once within the boundaries of the OT, no patient may walk, they are always passive objects.

It is considered imperative that a nurse from the patient's ward comes with the patient. She is in charge of the notes, and presumably will ensure the right patient gets the right operation. If a nurse is not available to conduct a patient, as has been seen above, theatre grinds to a halt. A shortage of porters also affects the turn-round time, and the length of a list often depends on the available porterage. In theory it is possible to operate on a 'conveyor belt' principle. When a surgeon is beginning to sew up a patient, he will inform the anaesthetist that the operation is coming to a conclusion. The anaesthetist will then ask a nurse to phone the ward for the next patient to be brought to theatre. In practice this does not obviate long gaps between patients – especially in plastic-surgery theatres where the anaesthetic induction is relatively long compared to the short minor operations carried out (see Chapter 3). Many other factors can lead to delays in patients arriving at theatre. The following extract from field notes describes a particularly slow morning in orthopaedic theatre.

2.27
[*10.30 a.m. There is a delay between patients.*]

ANAESTHETIC NURSE: Orthopaedic surgeons are the worst, they arrange things at the last minute, and then they're not organized properly.

RESEARCHER: Why is that?

A.N.: They don't communicate. It's probably because most of them are foreign – they don't understand each other.

[The delay continues. The registrar has been sent to look for a patient who cannot be found, but then is found in a different ward. In the meantime another patient has been added to the list – a 16-year-old accident victim, who has had his pelvis pinned a week earlier, and now is to have the pins out. However he has not been seen that day by the house doctor and he has not signed a consent form, and may not have been starved prior to general anaesthetic. The surgeon and registrar are not happy: the registrar is sent to the ward to sort things out.] *[Fifteen minutes later, the registrar returns.]*

REGISTRAR: He had been consented. The staff nurse thought the age of consent was 18, but he's signed himself. His father has been waiting around to sign a consent.

SURGEON [to researcher]: This is the sort of thing that happens. The consultant tells the staff nurse who tells the houseman, and the houseman forgets or is too busy.

[11.20 a.m. The patient finally arrives, and is very upset as he does not want a general anaesthetic after one the previous week had made him sick. Eventually he is persuaded by the surgeon, in the anaesthetic room.]

These delays seemed intractable at General, they are examined in detail in Chapter 5.

The patient is wheeled into the anaesthetic room on the trolley. In most OTs, this trolley, which brought the patient from the ward, will be used to move the patient into theatre, via the anaesthetic room. In thoracic OT, however, the patient is transferred once more while in the SC by the porter and the anaesthetist to a special sterile trolley kept within the OT confines, thus preventing the non-sterile trolley from entering the theatre itself. This additional separation of ward (non-sterile) from OT (sterile) in thoracic OT is a historical consequence of the original plan to use it for cardiac surgery, where sterility is considered paramount.

2.28

MR P.: The consultants, who were kings – gods rather – conned the administration into building thoracic theatres as cardiac theatres. But it was never used for cardiac surgery. Thoracic has no need of special sterile precautions, thoracic is pus, TB and infected lungs in cancer.

One of the theatres in this OT is now designated as a day case theatre, principally oral, plastic and other minor operations, and this special trolley is no longer used.

In the anaesthetic room no mention is made of the impending operation. The ward nurse talks to the patient while anaesthetist and assistant prepare the anaesthetic. The patient may have received a pre-operative sedative on the ward – this has a variable effect, some patients having to be woken up in order to be sure the general anaesthetic puts them to sleep. Because of the unpredictability of surgical lists, some patients not keeping appointments, others being admitted as urgent cases etc., a proportion of patients have not received pre-ops. These patients are usually less sanguine about the coming operation.

2.29
[*The patient (a boy of 16) is frightened because he does not want to have a general anaesthetic, having had a bad experience previously.*]
SURGEON [*intervenes*]: We won't give you gas, that's what you don't like isn't it.
[*Patient tearfully says he wants a local.*]
SURGEON MR K.: There isn't really a local anaesthetic that we can give for this. But we'll just give you an injection to send you to sleep.
[*Patient has no choice but to acquiesce.*]

The anaesthetist checks the case notes, which have been brought with the patient under her/his pillow. These will be the responsibility of the anaesthetist from now until the patient enters the recovery room, when they will be handed to recovery nursing staff. Based on patient weight, the dose of anaesthetic will be calculated. A cannula is inserted into a vein in the left index finger – this will be the access route to the patient's circulation in cases not requiring a drip. The syringe containing anaesthetic is attached to the cannula, and injected. As the anaesthetic is administered a veil of silence falls over all in the room. All focus their attention upon the eyes of the patient, as they close, and the anaesthetist checks for unconsciousness, tension evaporates. The blankets are whisked away, and put on a bench or work-surface – there does not seem to be a place set aside for them in the anaesthetic room – while the anaesthetist attaches a face mask to the patient, and connects a ventilator bag with which the patient's respiration is maintained until connected to an artificial ventilator in theatre; this bag is squeezed to breath the patient by the assistant or anaesthetic nurse. The ward nurse departs.

These processes may be summarized:

1 The patient is brought passively into the OT.
2 The patient is rendered unconscious.
3 The patient is rendered unable to breath, and dependent upon theatre personnel for life support.
4 The patient is stripped of clothes, and all vestiges of identity apart from a hospital bracelet and hospital notes. They constitute the separation of the patient from the outside world, completing the removal of a patient's identity which may have already undergone a degree of 'stripping', to adopt Goffman's (1968) term, in the period since hospitalization.

The anaesthetized patient is wheeled through the closed doors at the other end of the anaesthetic room into theatre. When moved to the trolley from a ward bed, a canvas sling has been placed under the patient, with two poles inserted into flaps on either side. By lifting these poles, the anaesthetist and assistant (or other handy personnel) can move the patient from the trolley to the operating table. The poles are removed, and placed on the trolley, which is wheeled through the doors on the right (i.e. not through the anaesthetic room) and left in the SC for the duration of the operation. This exercise may occasion comments on the weight of the patient, an apparently legitimate topic of personal comment while the patient is unconscious.

The anaesthetist now connects the patient to the artificial ventilator, and selects the anaesthetic to be used during the operation, which come as canisters of volatile agent attached to the mobile trolley. The patient's continued anaesthesia will thus be assured, and monitoring of the patient is now achieved by connection of ECG leads which provide pulse, respiration and heart rhythm information on a VDU mounted above the anaesthetic trolley. If a drip or blood products transfusion is anticipated by the surgeons, the anaesthetist will insert a cannula into a vein probably the median cubital vein inside the elbow.

While there is a cooperative atmosphere between most anaesthetist and surgeons, sometimes tension can occur at this point. The surgeons may be waiting, gowned and masked for the anaesthesia and preliminaries to be completed. The anaesthetist and any assistants congregate around the anaesthetic trolley, positioned near the patient's head. For thoracic, abdominal, or lower limb procedures, the surgeon stands on one side of the patient, with scrub nurse on her/his right, and an assistant opposite. Observers, including junior members of the surgical firm, stand where they can get a view, without threatening sterility. At the foot of the patient, or to one side, various equipment including a rack for used swabs, and possibly a bucket to collect blood drained from the operation site will be positioned, and the circulating nurse and any student nurses stand here. From this position they can see little of the operative technique but are able to observe the organization of operations, and learn how to service the surgeon. If the theatre sister is not the scrub nurse s/he may take a closer interest in the operation itself, and may enter into banter or conversation with the surgeons. The anaesthetic nurse also has more freedom to watch the surgery.

As was described earlier, the operation starts with the construction of a sterile field, entailing towelling over all but the immediate site of incision. Resection begins with the skin incision, which may be carried out by a junior member of the surgical team, who may also be invited to open the muscle layer in the case of abdominal surgery. Once the consultant or senior surgeon begins work, the focus of activity becomes the sterile field and the operative procedure. Although other activities are taking place (continuity of anaesthesia and monitoring, checking fluid loss, ordering blood products, arranging subsequent operations), these must not impinge upon the focus. Unscrubbed personnel must guard against contact with the sterile field, and be ready to move non-sterile equipment such as the microscope, lighting and stools for the surgeon.

There is a timeless quality to these periods – little happens which can be described other than the slow proceeding of the operation. The anaesthetist continues to monitor the patient and from time to time may make a note or speak briefly with the surgeon about the patient's condition. When surgery is minor then there may be conversation, and often the boredom is alleviated by banter or general conversation on matters of professional interest. During major surgery there is little conversation except between the surgeon and assistant.

Katz (1984) has suggested that the times of greatest tension in the operating room occurs at the boundaries, when the skin is broken or sewn, during anaesthesia. In her study, the operation itself was marked by low wit and chatter. My findings do not support this. Agreed, at the moment of anaesthesia there is a watchful silence, but when tension did develop during resection it was not during skin incision or closure. Perhaps there is a different tradition in the UK; my observations suggest that behaviour is restrained during the main part of an operation, and that extraneous talk is seen as highly threatening. Even the outspoken Mrs A. reserved her outbursts for before and after the operation itself. Disruption of this restraint was strictly punished on one occasion:

2.30
SURGEON MR M. [*demonstrating blunt dissection to assistant, with house doctor looking on*]: Now you put your finger in there; don't go any further. But you see how far you can go with blunt dissection. If I had used a piece of metal in there we'd have done some trouble.
SENIOR REGISTRAR: Winkle it?
HOUSE OFFICER [*barely audible*]: Very Freudian.
MR M. [*sharply*]: Psychiatry you're going in for is it? [*pause*] We don't say that.
HOUSE OFFICER: No . . . It's just something I've heard.

This imputation of a sexual equivalence to surgical activity was 'dirty', and out of place in the operating theatre. It was punished by a worse insult: a future in psychiatry.

The proceedings conducted during this phase are characterized by the patient's dependence on others for her/his existence. In this dangerous condition the surgical patient lies naked and unconscious, reduced to so much meat, oblivious to time, physical changes and pain. Her/his identity is defined only by a plastic tag around the wrist, and the name of the operative procedure written on a board in the theatre.

When the operation has been completed, and the skin suture begun, the surgeon informs the anaesthetist that the operation is over. The latter will now time the ending of anaesthesia to coincide with the completion, by administering oxygen to awaken the patient. Dressings are supervised by the consultant surgeon but often applied by assistant surgeon. Surgeons then depart, and used equipment is cleared away. Monitoring equipment is detached, an antidote to the muscle relaxant (if used) is administered, and the patient is lifted on to the trolley, which has been brought back into theatre. A blanket is placed over the patient, and s/he is addressed by the anaesthetist, 'Wake up [name] . . ., it's all over' and is asked to cough: s/he once again has an identity. The patient is made to say something, to assert his/her agency, but most likely will then go back to sleep for a considerable time. The patient is wheeled out of theatre by the anaesthetist and assistant, via the side doors, into the recovery room, where nursing staff are continually present to observe the patient. The anaesthetist checks the patient's pulse and hands the notes written up during the operation with details of heart rate, respiration, and the drugs given, to the recovery nurse.

The recovery space is still within the OT boundary, and seems to possess characteristics of a half-way house for those who work there.

2.31
NURSE A.: They [ward nurses] don't like you in recovery. You're in between.
NURSE ANAESTHETIST: You're definitely in-between.

Ward nurses who go to collect a patient from the OT are contaminated too.

2.32
NURSE B.: When you bring a patient back from theatre, the other nurses say 'over there'. We were taught that you welcome a patient back. After all, they've been to theatre.

While in recovery, the anaesthetist retains authority over the patient, deciding when s/he can return to the ward, or occasionally, be moved to Intensive Therapy Unit (ITU). The surgeon has authority only when the patient is on the table, the anaesthetist oversees the induction and recovery periods.

2.33
A patient had been operated on for a brain tumour, and was in recovery. The anaesthetist Dr A. was called to recovery an hour after the operation was complete, and having conducted blood pressure and ECG tests returned to theatre to tell surgeon Mr C. that the patient 'was a bit flat'. He suspected a sub-arachnoid bleed which was threatening life by putting pressure on the brain, and summoned the surgeon, fully scrubbed, to recovery to assess the requirement for re-operation. The surgeon agreed with the diagnosis and an emergency procedure was instigated.

Thus a patient who was apparently moving out of the surgical space in a 'healed' condition, was returned for further surgery, and it was only after a second operation that healing was finally complete, and the patient moved to ITU, and eventually to a ward. Patients in ITU are the responsibility of an anaesthetist, although surgeons' post-operative rounds will obviously include patients in Intensive Therapy.

Discussion

In the latter part of the chapter, the movements performed by patients during surgery have been described in detail, and the process of resection, which makes surgery unique among healing activities, has been placed in the wider context of the overall process by which a patient is conducted through the surgical space. Clearly resection marks the biophysical means whereby disease is confronted by the surgeon, and with her/his skill excised or removed partially or wholly. This process is given due weight, and the proceedings in the OT have as their focus the times when this activity is underway. At these times, all else is seen as tangential. Yet, the successful achievement of resection must also depend on its adjuncts, the techniques of sterility and anaesthesia.

As far as the first of these goes, the circuits of hygiene ensure that the patient arrives at the moment when resection begins in a condition which is intended to ensure that the operation does not unintentionally increase the 'illness' of the patient through infection. S/he is washed, sterile towels draped, skin disinfected. Instruments are sterilized, and the people who are to wield them have undergone routines to ensure that as far as possible they do not introduce infective agents into the wound. These procedures are time-consuming, yet they are recognized as essentials. Corners cannot be cut, and the routines are accepted by all involved as legitimate uses of staff time and resources.

The circuits of hygiene thus bring together patient, instruments and surgical staff in one place, in conditions which minimize the risks that resection brings to a patient. Not only do they achieve this, but they assure that they are *seen* to have been achieved. The circuits mark the efforts of all to make surgery a safe procedure, one which will not increase disease, a circumstance which would be hard to match with the idea of surgery as a form of *healing*.

Because of the necessity for sterile preparations to be achieved without fault, the surgeon is dependent on the rest of the team to ensure that the patient comes to her/his knife in a 'hygienic' condition (hygiene[2]). Surgeons do not oversee the entire procedure, which from the early morning washing of the OT floors with disinfectant are aimed to achieve asepsis, or some approximation to it. They retire to their office, they let the theatre staff get the theatre to its state of readiness for resection to occur. During the fieldwork, impatience by surgeons during these preparation periods was never witnessed (compare this with the impatience demonstrated with regard to anaesthetic time in Chapter 3). In the latter stages, surgeons are involved themselves, in scrubbing, and in overseeing the preparation of the patient. Even though the direct intervention by the surgeon is limited to the resection, the point at which s/he takes responsibility for the patient is as soon as s/he arrives on the operating table (this leads to a particularly interesting situation in neurosurgery OT, as will be seen in Chapter 3). Responsibility is returned to the anaesthetist after the wound has been dressed, at which point the circuits of hygiene resume, with the moving of patient, dirty instruments, etc.

The circuits of hygiene are central to the team effort of surgery. The surgeon relies on all in the OT to co-operate in the enterprise. The circuits routinize these efforts, they remove responsibility from the surgeon for overseeing the entire proceedings, and assure her/him that all has been done to enable healing to take place safely. Hygiene[2], the requisite for surgery to be healing, depends on routines of hygiene[1] carried out by theatre staff, over whom the surgeon has no direct control. Yet, when the surgeon approaches the operating table, the rhetoric of the circuits of hygiene assure her/him that all has been done according to the law of asepsis.

To conclude, the description of the complex routines of surgery in this chapter has indicated ways in which the surgeon depends on collaborative efforts for the success of surgery. Her/his reputation as a healer depends on activities which others must perform. The routines of asepsis, which since their innovation have been claimed as rituals, demonstrate to surgeons that they may operate with maximum certitude that their intervention will not endanger the patient by infection. The success or failure of surgical resection will depend entirely on the surgeon's skill. The surgeon's authority will be achieved by dint of her/his clinical skill and judgement in treating the disease of her/his patients. By opposing skill on one hand to routine or even ritual (irrational), the surgical discourse negates the very efforts which s/he depends on – the circuits of hygiene – in order to make her/his claims to be a healer.

The issue of the social relations of the surgical team, and how it is constituted, will continue as a theme of this book, which will turn in the next chapter to consider the relationship between surgeon and anaesthetist, and in Chapter 5, which examines the management of the OT, to the relations between clinicians, nurses and managers.

Commentary

It will not have escaped the attention of many readers that the procedures which have been described in this chapter have the characteristics of what has been called the *rite de passage* (Gennep, 1960), with its three stages of separation, liminal transition and re-integration. *Rites de passage* have been identified in pre-industrial societies, and the theory has been developed in the work of many anthropologists including Turner (1968, 1969) and Douglas (1984), while Bocock (1974) suggests that they are also present in many Western ceremonies which mark transitions of status. A non-functionalist analysis which identifies the use of rituals in constituting the authority of the powerful has been developed by La Fontaine (1977), and this approach perhaps helps to move the notion of the *rite de passage* beyond the impression, following Gluckman (1962, p. 9), that all the theory says is that things have a beginning, a middle and an end. In this reading, rituals appear to effect status transition in their subjects, but their actual achievement is the validation of the knowledge of the authorities who institute the *rites*. Weddings validate the authority of religious orders to define social relations between men and women; retirement parties legitimate the power of employers to sack their sexagenarians.

A different reading to the one developed in this chapter would consider the *rite de passage* as a model of what is happening in surgery. Anthropologists distinguish between the instrumental and the symbolic or 'ritual', and the circuits of hygiene possess many characteristics of rituals of separation, liminality and re-integration. Gennep emphasizes that the *rite* has a social, not an individual function. In this structuralist reading, the routines of the OT serve to move a patient from a dangerous social state to a safe one, as someone who is healed. The authority of the surgeon is allocated to her/him as the agent by which this change of status is effected. The ritual clothing has many characteristics in common with that of other officiators at *rites de passage*: clergy, judges, Black Rod. The high status of surgery derives from its possession of these ritual attributes, which other healing specialties do not have.

3

SURGEONS AND ANAESTHETISTS

Introduction

It is usual in Western medical care for one doctor of consultant or equivalent rank to manage and take responsibility for each patient. Occasionally, for instance when a patient's condition involves more than one specialty, responsibility may be shared. However, there is one situation in which joint management of a case is institutionalized. That situation is the surgical operating theatre. For the duration of the patient's sojourn in this arena of care, s/he is under the management of two consultants: a surgeon and an anaesthetist.

This dual responsibility is one of a number of distinctive features of surgery. The routinized technique of anaesthesia stands alongside the sterile technology of the operating theatre and the extreme interventionism of the specialty to distinguish surgery as a form of healing. This chapter considers the relationship between surgeons and anaesthetists within the operating theatre suite (OT). The deconstructive methodology will be used to demonstrate how the division of labour within the OT between these two specialties can be understood as two quite different perspectives upon their patient. By recognizing that these differences are institutionalized in the discourse of the specialties, it is then possible to understand conflict between surgeons and anaesthetists, conflict which is usually resolved, but on occasions which is sustained, with potentially disastrous consequences for patients.

This clinical double-act of surgeon and anaesthetist contributes an important element of the surgical discourse, marking what is being done to a patient as a procedure in her/his best interest, a healing of disease, despite the signs that suggest the contrary which are the consequence of the radical nature of surgery. The rhetoric of anaesthesia constitutes the surgical patient as a subject in a way which no other healing specialty, including surgery itself, can, and assists in supplying surgery with its authority to heal.

The material in this chapter, as with that throughout this work is drawn from the study of elective surgery, principally at General Hospital. In an alien environment such as the OT, key informants are particularly valuable. If the ideal informant is the native speaker who (while a player in the field) is just distant enough to also wish to accommodate an attractive relationship with the researcher, then the surgeon is a far from ideal informant. They are centre stage, and wish to draw the researcher into their activities. I have documented how an observer became a participant at various points in this book. The anaesthetist is a far better informant.

The watchfulness of the anaesthetist during surgical procedures induces in some the role of naive anthropologist, although in others it engenders cynicism or disinterest. I was fortunate to discover a number in the former category, whose assistance and information throughout the fieldwork was invaluable. As will be seen, the key concept in the analysis of the observational data upon the relationship between surgeon and anaesthetist was derived directly from a remark by anaesthetist and principal informant Dr J., although its significance at the time was not fully appreciated.

The structure of this chapter is as follows. The first section describes the division of labour within the OT deriving from a detailed case study. I then document anaesthetists' own responses to their relationship with surgeons, and from this develop an organizing principle by which the perspectives of surgeon and anaesthetist upon the patient may be understood. Deconstruction of these perspectives shows how the discourses, while rival, act symbiotically for the majority of interactions. The last section of the chapter examines three other detailed case studies of surgical operations, which reflect the range of different interactions possible between surgeon and anaesthetist. These demonstrate the contradictory discourses of surgeon and anaesthetist, the points of conflict between these discourses, the mutual advantage which the two specialties derive from their symbiosis, and the possibilities of this symbiosis failing.

The division of labour within the OT

Within the operating theatre, the two clinical specialties of surgeon and anaesthetist come into contact. The different phases of patient passage through the OT have been described in Chapter 2, and the interactions with anaesthetists and surgeons noted. However, the interaction *between* these categories of clinician have not been spelt out. This can most simply be done by reference to a case study, which will document the input of both specialties to the process of resection.

Case study 1: arterial graft

Location: General Theatres N
Surgeon: Mr M.
Anaesthetist: Dr J.
Scrub Nurse Sister: G.
Assisting surgeon Senior Registrar S.; two surgical house officers
Anaesthetic nurse J.; four theatre nurses; also present ambulance-man trainee, researcher

The patient is a 58-year-old male undergoing aortic bifemoral graft for aortic aneurysm.

[9 a.m.] The patient is brought to general theatres and enters the anaesthetic room accompanied by a nurse from his ward. The anaesthetist Dr J. has visited the patient the previous evening, and a pre-med has been administered to the patient on the ward. The patient has no history which would suggest risk from general anaesthesia. He is suffering from a large aortic aneurysm (a collapse of the elasticity of the wall of the main artery of the body) as a result of atheroma (a build up of canary-yellow fatty deposit which partially occludes the aorta, increasing pressure on the walls of the vessel). The atheroma extends to the junctions with the two femoral arteries and replacement of the affected aorta and tops of the femoral arteries with a synthetic graft is necessary to avoid either rupture of the aorta and/or thrombosis in the lower limb vessels caused by atheroma and blood clot breaking away.

Dr J. had been informed of the case the previous week:

3.1
Mr M. was completing a case in general theatres. He turned to Dr J.: 'Oh by the way, we have another of those bi-fems next week.' Dr J. asks for brief details, then turns to the researcher: 'You should really be here to see that case, it will take up the whole morning list.' He then describes the procedure to the researcher.

There was no question that the procedure would take place, even though no anaesthetist had at that time seen the patient. The information appeared to be given only so that Dr J. would know well in advance of this major case.

Anaesthesia was administered to the patient by a cannula inserted into the left forefinger. A cocktail of anaesthetic and muscle relaxant (curare) was given, and the usual silence fell as the patient's eyes flickered and closed. Immediately, a mask was attached over the patient's nose and mouth, and gaseous agent and oxygen administered, the assistant squeezing a rubber bag to artificially breath the now-paralysed patient. The patient was then wheeled into theatre, and connected to the ventilator on the anaesthetic trolley. Because of the length of the procedure (3–4 hours), complex monitoring was required, and in addition to the normal sensors which measure pulse rate and blood pressure, electrodes were attached to the patient to provide an ECG trace, plus sensors to blood vessels in the neck connected to measure venous and arterial blood pressure. A cannula was inserted into the median cubital vein (inside the elbow) and a drip attached to provide access to the patient's circulation for saline, plasma or whole blood. Dr J. had also brought into the theatre in a large old bag (which stood out against the gleaming sterile furnishing) a piece of non-standard equipment, an automatic syringe infuser. The researcher questioned him:

3.2

RESEARCHER: Does this extra gear come from the department?

DR J.: It belongs to me, well, it belongs to the Department of Anaesthetics. The reason I have it is because I'm running a trial of a particular drug for a company, and they provided the machine. The department couldn't afford it, well they could afford it, but . . . . I looked at this particular drug, and thought it would be a good one to infuse by syringe infuser.

This equipment was used automatically to inject a measured dose of relaxant into the patient throughout the long operation, thereby ensuring that satisfactory surgical access to the abdomen would be maintained. Dr J. was setting this up while the patient was draped with towels and prepared for surgery. The anaesthetist thus had an impressive array of technology upon which to monitor the condition of the unconscious patient. The skin incision began at approximately 9.30 a.m., and once the operation began, the anaesthetist seated himself so he could observe the various monitors. Every 10 minutes he marked readings in the patient's charts, which are kept on the anaesthetic trolley for the duration of the operation. Only at one point, when the synthetic graft was being sewn in place, did Dr J. move to a position where he could observe the wound, which he did briefly, and mainly apparently to look at the level of blood loss. The other members of the surgical and anaesthetic teams took more interest in the resection, which was not a run-of-the-mill operation, and thus broke the usual tedium of minor surgery.

In order to assess the respective responsibilities of surgeon and anaesthetist within the surgical team, a number of events during the operation will be documented.

1 After dissecting down to the aorta, it was discovered that the organ was diseased to a higher level than had been thought, and it was necessary to dissect out the vessel further than had been intended and into a more inaccessible position. The surgeon informed the anaesthetist, as it entailed an increase in operation time. [10.50 a.m.] The anaesthetist was also informed when the aorta was clamped before resection. This was because clamping would affect measurement of blood pressure artificially and it was necessary that the anaesthetist did not respond inappropriately. [11.30 a.m.]

2 The period when the aorta was clamped was the most critical, as no blood could reach the lower limbs during this period. The anaesthetist's concern to ensure that no permanent damage resulted from the operation was greatest during this period, and Dr J. was highly vigilant of any contraindication, and

when a phone-call for him was relayed by a nurse, he said he was unable to leave the theatre and would call back.

3 The synthetic graft material is initially permeable, and once sewn in place at the top must have blood leaked through it to render it impermeable as the blood clots on the graft material. Blood pressure during this phase fell dramatically, and the surgeon mentioned that the clotting was not taking place quickly, 'I'm afraid there's rather a lot of blood in here'. Dr J. quickly put up a unit of plasma on the drip and wrote a prescription for four units of blood, which was then sent to the transfusion service in the hospital by porter. During this period [11.50 a.m.] a low blood pressure alarm was sounding on a monitor, after a while this alarm (but not the monitor) was turned off to reduce the sense of anxiety this was generating.

4 Mr M. sewed one of the graft 'legs' to a femoral artery, and then supervised his Senior Registrar S. on the other side. However the consequent anastomosis (join) was not blood-tight and the sewing had to be cut and re-done by Mr M. Dr J. was kept informed of developments. [12.25 a.m.] After this repair, and with the clamp removed to allow circulation to be restored, a further small amount of bleeding was found still to be occurring. Eventually it was decided that the leakage was from the top end of the graft, which was very inaccessible. As it could not be further repaired it was decided to leave it, with the expectation that clot would form eventually. Bearing in mind the length of the operation, now some 4 hours, the surgeon and anaesthetist agreed that a drain should be inserted into the abdominal cavity and the patient be sewn up and brought out of anaesthesia.

5 Dr J. was concerned to ensure that blood loss was replaced. A minor problem had occurred when only two units of blood were immediately available, and at one point plasma had to be substituted. Toward the end of the operation Dr J. concerned himself with complex attempts to gauge the extent of blood loss which had occurred. This entailed collecting and measuring all liquid drained from the operation site, and weighing blood-soaked swabs. In this way a rough guide to blood loss was obtained, although Dr J. told the researcher that the method was 'considerably inaccurate'. As soon as this had been done, the nursing staff concerned themselves with the ritual of counting of swabs and instruments to ensure nothing was left in the wound.

6 While the skin suture was being completed, the anaesthetist administered the antidote to the curarizing agent. The wound dressed and the patient transferred to the trolley, oxygen was given and the patient brought to consciousness. Once he had been seen to be awake he was moved to recovery. The operation has been long and traumatic, and the patient subsequently was transferred to the Intensive Therapy Unit (ITU), under the care of the anaesthetist and specialist nursing staff.

In this case study, which has been described in detail, the patient was diagnosed as possessing a serious condition which required surgery. The patient was also sufficiently fit to cope with the trauma of the operation. Throughout the procedure the surgeon had authority to dictate the course of events, and his wishes took precedence over that of the anaesthetist. The problems caused by the failure of anastomosis compromised the patient's fitness seriously however, and the operation was concluded in some haste, on the advice of the anaesthetist. Despite being moved to Intensive Therapy, the operation was considered 'successful'. Although a possibility remained that the patient would succumb from shock to the vascular system and loss of blood, the aneurysm had been successfully resected and replaced.

Throughout the operation, the anaesthetist was acting as *proxy* for the patient. His ability to breath was under the control of the anaesthetist, and his heart rate and blood pressure was monitored and manipulated chemically during the procedure. When the operation was stressing the patient, sapping his capacity to survive the strain put on his constitution by the surgery, blood loss, and anaesthetic agents, the anaesthetist acted to moderate this loss, conserving enough fitness to see the patient through the operation. The anaesthetist, on behalf of the patient, antagonized the surgeon's actions which were having the effect of *injuring* the patient at the same time as removing his disease. Later in the chapter I will return to this issue of a patient's complement of *fitness*, which s/he possesses alongside the *illness* for which surgery is being conducted, and these opposing principles will be seen to be important parts of surgical and anaesthetic discourse.

Having described this case, it is now appropriate to look for some simple rules of the division of labour between surgeon and anaesthetist within the OT, deriving from the fieldwork observations.

1 The division of labour between anaesthetist and surgeon defines certain spatial arrangements in the OT. As noted in Chapter 2, in some suites anaesthetists and surgeons have different methods of gaining access to the theatre, the anaesthetist through the anaesthetic room, the surgeon through the scrub area.

   3.3
   The surgeon and anaesthetist were talking in the sterile corridor. The patient was wheeled into the anaesthetic room. The surgeon moved into the scrub room, and the anaesthetist held the door of the scrub room ajar while they finished their conversation. Then he went back into the SC and entered the anaesthetic room through its separate entrance.

2 The patient's head will normally be the domain of the anaesthetist. The anaesthetic trolley is positioned so that gaseous anaesthetics may be accessed to the face mask; all connections to pulse, respiration and electrocardiogram (ECG) monitors are routed under the head pillow. Often a wall of sterile towelling will be erected to separate the operation site from the domain of

the anaesthetist. It may also serve, if a patient is not under general anaesthesia, to prevent possible intervention by the patient.

3.4
A patient was to have needle marks removed from her forearm by means of a high-speed drill attachment which scoured the superficial layers of skin. This procedure was done using a local anaesthetic. The patient was extremely distressed by the noise and (non-painful but strange) sensation of contact with the instrument. She was prevented from seeing the procedure by means of a wall of towelling between the operation site and her head, the anaesthetic team talked to her during the short procedure to distract her from the operation.

Where the surgeon requires access to the head of the patient conflict of interests may arise. For example, during a bronchoscopy, general anaesthesia cannot be provided by gaseous agents. In this situation, the surgeon's right of access to the patient's head take precedence, and the anaesthetist has to find a new means of administering anaesthetic such as continuous intravenous injection.

3 The instrumentation concerning the patient's condition is the province of the anaesthetist, and the surgeon is not expected to initiate comment on the readings, and indeed is assumed not to be able to decipher them. This is an important element in anaesthetist discourse; as one put it:

3.5
ANAESTHETIST DR J.: The surgeon is a technical person trained to do carpentry, with some background knowledge of how the system works. At some point there is a need for the technical knowledge of the anaesthetist; it's a technical field with use of equipment which anaesthetists understand because of their interest. Surgeons do not understand the machinery.

Anaesthetists argue that they take clinical decisions based on their technical knowledge:

3.6
DR J.: We are applied physiologists and pharmacologists as well as physicians.

This assumed technical superiority of anaesthetists is one way that closure is achieved in the OT.

3.7
DR J.: Historically anaesthesia started as a 'Cinderella' specialty; it was not regarded as prestigious, but as a joke. There was no training, and was therefore not attractive to join. But anaesthetists have realized the value of their skill, and have made sure they have been able to

communicate it to other people. They have put training high up in priorities.

The anaesthetist will inform the surgeon if any monitor indicates deviation from a norm, for instance low blood pressure. The anaesthetist in effect 'interprets' the technical data for the benefit of the surgeon, who is then expected to act upon it.

4 Similarly, a surgeon will inform the anaesthetist if a complication has arisen, for instance a bleed or an expectation of lengthened operation duration. In both interactions the recipient in the communication is allowed to 'diagnose' from the 'symptom' reported to her/him. An anaesthetist would not be expected to comment on the state of the operation directly.

3.8

During the anastomosis the surgeon Mr M. commented to the anaesthetist, 'I'm afraid there is rather a lot of blood in here', rather than saying that a transfusion was needed. The anaesthetist, immediately 'wrote up' a further two units of plasma and sent his assistant to collect them from the blood bank, while busying himself with checking the various monitors of the patient's condition.

5 During operations, social interaction occurs within surgical and anaesthetic teams, but rarely between teams. Even when surgeons and anaesthetists are well-known to each other, little association occurs, conversation often being limited to technical queries and information. Anaesthetists may occasionally move so they can watch the surgical procedure, but when seeking a good vantage point are not accorded any right of seniority by more junior members of the surgical team. They do not make any comments on the state of surgical activity. Outside the theatre, anaesthetists and surgeons were observed to interact freely, as would be expected for senior colleagues in a work place.

6 As described in Chapter 2, the surgeon will control proceedings only for the period while the patient is on the operating table. Having had responsibility for the patient up to this point, once on the table the surgeon may give instructions how the patient is to be positioned and prepared, and the anaesthetic team will carry out these instructions. The end of the period is defined by the completion of wound dressing. Outside this period, responsibility for the patient lies with the anaesthetist. No observations indicated that there was any ambiguity over the definition of these boundaries of responsibility, but there were variants worth noting.

3.9

A patient was brought into the neurosurgery anaesthetic room on a ward trolley. She was transferred directly on to the operating table, which had been moved into the room. The surgeon entered once the patient had been anaesthetized, and attached the head clamp to the end of the table, and then positioned the patient's head in the clamp to prevent any movement during the operation. During this procedure there was discussion between surgeon and anaesthetist of the forthcoming operation.

In this particular instance important information about the history of the patient, expectations for the coming operation and possible complications were routinely communicated. Neurosurgery is a sub-specialty in which uncertainty, both of diagnosis and prognosis will tend to be high, and this may start to explain the greater level of interaction between surgeon and anaesthetist. Having entered the anaesthetist's territory, the surgeon was involving the anaesthetist in the intended management of the patient.

In general, surgeon–anaesthetist interaction was a source of interest during the fieldwork precisely because the encounter appeared to be carried off so successfully despite minimal actual communication. Dr J. suggested that this could largely be put down to 'experience', by which both parties learn how much input from each is needed for particular procedures. The highly stylized courtesy of surgeon–anaesthetist interaction is reminiscent of Strong's description of mother–physician interaction in a paediatric clinic (Strong, 1978) which he argued enabled participants to carry off a successful encounter despite their unequal status, and different but equally legitimate rights over the child as patient-object. To develop this analogy, it would therefore be reasonable to suggest that the surgeon and the anaesthetist hold differing, though equally legitimate definitions of the patient. I will look first at the clinical decisions made by anaesthetists with regard to their patients.

The anaesthetist's decision

The original decision to admit a patient for a particular elective surgical procedure will have been taken by a surgeon in out-patient clinic, based on clinical judgement of diagnosis and prognosis, severity of condition and history. Patients will therefore be admitted for surgery principally on an assessment of the particular problem presenting.

3.10
SURGEON MR P.: We [surgeons] make up the list. The admissions department will pull patients off a waiting list, which has been vetted by me to ensure that it contains patients which are suitable.

Decisions over what kind of anaesthesia to employ are taken at a later stage, usually only after the patient has been admitted to hospital. This in itself may be a source of tension between the specialties, as will be seen. For any surgical procedure, there will be ground rules which define appropriate anaesthetic technique. Two differing objectives are behind the use of anaesthetic agents in the OT; firstly the prevention of pain (analgesia) during and after an operation, secondly the achievement of unconsciousness. There is a degree of overlap between these objectives, and the technologies of the anaesthetist are necessarily complex, and beyond the scope of this book or my technical knowledge. Briefly, analgesics will normally be administered by means of injection of agent, either locally, or by means of a 'block', the prevention of sensation distally by the use of anaesthetic agent to interrupt the transmission of nervous impulses by a nerve or nerve plexus between the area to be desensitized and the central nervous system. The most common blocks are brachial (upper limb), femoral (lower limb) and spinal and epidural blocks (roughly below the level of the injection, for abdominal and occasionally thoracic procedures.) These will last longer than general anaesthetics, and are used when a high level of pain control after operation is required.

General anaesthetics also provide a degree of analgesia, but are principally used to achieve unconsciousness. Since the 1940s, agents such as curare have been used as muscle relaxants, permitting lower and thus safer levels of general anaesthetic to be used. The level of anaesthesia achieved must therefore be carefully monitored, to ensure analgesia and unconsciousness throughout the surgical procedure, as a curarised patient would (while being artificially respirated) be unable to indicate a return of sensation (Mushin, 1948; Hewer, 1953; Churchill-Davidson, 1984). General anaesthesia will usually be induced in patients by means of an intravenous agent, it will then be sustained by gaseous agents. Post-operative analgesia is limited, and once in recovery patients may require pain control.

Anaesthetists thus have considerable opportunities to make decisions about the type of anaesthetic agent to be used in a particular surgical circumstance. Their technical knowledge will be employed to ensure that, in their opinion, an appropriate method of anaesthesia is utilised. This decision will in general be based on three criteria:

1 The nature of the surgical procedure.
2 The physiological status and history of the surgical subject.
3 The social circumstances of the surgical subject.

The anaesthetist will thus seek to make a clinical judgement about the patient based on assessment of these criteria. Surgical procedures often suggest a particular form of anaesthetic, some are appropriate for a general, others for a block, etc. However, the physiology and social circumstances of patients may necessitate deviation from these ground rules, and it is in these areas that anaesthetists claim their right to exercise control over patient passage through surgery. During the fieldwork, informants provided many examples of how these deviations are assessed. For example, young children are often intractable during surgery except under general anaesthesia, and patients over 70 years have increased risk of cardiac or respiratory complications and may be considered unsuitable cases for general anaesthetics. Decisions as to what anaesthetic is to be employed in these cases are made by an anaesthetist, usually as a result of a visit to the ward the evening previous to surgery. Consultation with the patient's consultant surgeon, who from experience will know a good deal about the kind of patient who may require non-standard anaesthesia, may also have taken place, as may other interventions.

3.11
A patient Mr H. who had been called for surgery for inguinal hernia and fistula was informed by a house doctor, on admission, that he might have to have his operation under spinal anaesthesia, a possibility he confided to the researcher he anticipated with considerable anxiety. Two conflicting pieces of information were contributing to uncertainty: a history of ischaemic heart disease (IHD) had led to his GP suggesting he was unsuitable for general anaesthetic, while a consultant anaesthetist six years previously had used a general, and no further IHD symptoms had subsequently presented. The final decision was to be made by a consultant anaesthetist who was to visit the patient and take a history and examination later in the evening before the operation.

There is also considerable leeway within the main categories of anaesthesia for anaesthetists to 'tailor' agents to particular patients. For example, a record of which agents were used during surgery is made, and if a patient has a subsequent operation a different agent will be employed, as this will reduce the likelihood of respiratory irritation, allergy or other complications.

3.12
DR J.: If a patient has had a previous operation, then we will usually use a different anaesthetic agent to that used the last time. They all have slightly different side effects and this reduces the risk of idiosyncratic response.

Social circumstances also affect choice of agent, principally in relation to recovery from anaesthesia. Patients who can be made comfortable at home, or have familial commitments may be selected for blocks more readily. Surgeons are expected to take social circumstances into account, but this seemed to be a very *ad hoc* procedure. A memorandum circulated by anaesthetists concerning suitability of patients for day surgery indicated that accompaniment home should be arranged, that they should live within 20 miles of the hospital. Being male and having female kin appeared to make the use of non-general anaesthesia more likely. These assessments are worthy of further research.

Anaesthetic discourse is thus concerned with these decisions, which are outside the realm of the surgeon. Even when no particular history or social circumstance indicated non-standard anaesthesia, it was observed that particular anaesthetists favour certain agents, or like to use non-standard equipment during certain surgical procedures. Anaesthetists are inveterate innovators, taking advantage of any opportunity such as an offer from a drug company to test new agents or equipment. To further examine the nature of anaesthetic discourse, anaesthetists are now given the opportunity to speak for themselves.

Anaesthetists talking about surgeons

3.13
DR J.: There has always been a love–hate relationship between anaesthetists and surgeons.

During the period of fieldwork, anaesthetists were particularly valuable informants. Partly this was due to the spatial arrangements of the theatre, close to the anaesthetist's trolley being a good place to stand, out of the way and generally ignored. Secondly, anaesthetists often have long periods of virtual inactivity, punctuated only by occasional note-taking, during which only a deviation from norms will instigate any activity. They were therefore usually very happy to break with the tedium to talk to the researcher. As a result, these 'naive anthropologists' in the OT provided the researcher with many useful insights into the social organization of surgery. They were particularly forthcoming on their perceived superiority to surgeons.

Anaesthetists and surgeons are based in different hospital departments, with their own internal secretarial and administrative support, their own hierarchies and their own internal political concerns. As individuals, consultant anaesthetists and surgeons may have private practice and membership of other bodies both clinical and non-clinical. However, in the OT, these two autonomous specialties come into close contact, and are highly dependent upon each other. The comment of one informant, the anaesthetist Dr C., that 'surgeons need anaesthetists, and anaesthetists would have no work without surgeons', while perhaps obvious, is of interest here, for it will inscribe at an interpersonal level the symbiotic aspects of the relationship between individual anaesthetists and surgeons. Symbiosis, as with any dependency, need not of course be uncritical, as the reference by Dr J. (see above) of surgeons as technically competent in 'carpentry', suggests. A major source of irritation for anaesthetists appears to be effectively in-built in the administration of elective surgery, whereby referrals from GPs to surgeons do not concurrently lead to an anaesthetic consultation prior to admission:

3.14
DR J.: A patient goes to the GP, who identifies a problem and refers the patient to the surgeon of his preference, most likely as a result of the old-boy network rather than any thoughts about waiting lists. How patients are sent for [from waiting lists] is up to the surgeon. Sometimes, rarely, a date will be fixed at the out-patient appointment and put in the diary, but at the other end of the spectrum, the surgeon's secretary determines who comes in off the waiting list. Or a consultant may plan

lists at the beginning of the week, and state which cases he wants to see. Then when a patient is admitted, he is seen by nurses, then a junior doctor who will do investigations, but unlikely any which they might think the anaesthetist will need.

Patients may thus be admitted who are quite unsuited to surgery because of their being at high risk from general anaesthesia, or may be put on a list without recognition of the long induction time associated with non-general techniques such as epidural anaesthesia.

3.15

DR J.: Surgeons assume that there is nothing wrong with a patient apart from what they are having the operation for. But this may not be the case, and must be identified. There may be consequences of the treatment for the anaesthetist, because while a surgeon is interested in the patient in terms of the abnormality, the rest of the patient is of interest to the anaesthetist. Two to three per cent of patients will have a problem which cannot be sorted out in advance, and in these cases your choices are either to hope for the best, or to cancel the operation, or initiate further investigations. But some of these could have been done by the GP, or by the surgeon, or could have been done if an earlier admission had been arranged.

As a consequence, it is usually only after a patient has been admitted for surgery, probably the previous day, that an anaesthetist will have an opportunity to assess a patient:

3.16

DR J.: An anaesthetist should see the patient, or should at least be informed about the patient by the house doctor. The anaesthetist can contact the surgical departmental secretary to find out who is on the list, or wait till five-thirty on the day previous to a list, when it is pinned up, but some surgical firms will not have been able to concoct a list till the morning of the schedule, and it is very difficult to get details of the list which may indicate problems.

This particular informant was strongly critical of surgeons' inability to put together a list which fitted into a three-hour session. The comments reported here were made against a backcloth of a particularly chaotic week in plastic-surgery theatre during which patients had been scheduled to be in theatre hours before they were admitted, and two major cases had been scheduled for an afternoon session and had had to be rearranged. During a lull of some 40 minutes while a patient was given a pre-med and transported to theatre, I was invited into a linen store in which a catalogue of apparent incompetence of surgical organization was recounted by the anaesthetist and the theatre sister. These data are examined in greater detail in Chapter 5. This allusion to incompetence is, however, restricted to ability to administer:

3.17

DR J.: Anaesthetists are well organized, surgeons tend to be less well-organized; they can rely on junior staff; when hell breaks out, it breaks out very quickly. It's a problem having to think for everyone. You suppose that everyone knows what they are doing, but much of the time they don't seem to. Anaesthetists perhaps are in a better position than most to have an overview.

The administrative incompetence imputed to surgeons is greatest when it directly affects anaesthetists, as it does over the time taken in the anaesthetic induction of the patient, a major source of irritation on both sides.

3.18

ANAESTHETIST DR C.: The surgeons don't consider the anaesthesia to be anything other than time wasted, and do not seem to calculate for it when they make up a list. They don't take any interest in the anaesthetic, even though they depend on it. We have to have the patient ready when they want it. I was in the US; there if you say it will take an hour to prepare a patient, the surgeon will go to his office for an hour, and do some paperwork.

3.19

DR J.: However a list is made up, directly or from a waiting list, it is a real problem for the smooth running of surgery that surgeons will think of the operating time but will forget the anaesthetic and induction time.

Consequently, at the end of the induction, the surgeons may be waiting, gowned and masked for the anaesthesia and preliminaries to be completed.

3.20

As the patient was slipping into unconsciousness, the consultant surgeon Mr F. peered in through the anaesthetic room window. All the nurses immediately pulled up their masks, stood stiffly erect, and pulled open the doors to the theatre. The anaesthetist Dr C. murmured to the researcher, 'Did you see that'?

One anaesthetist, who was a local general practitioner who came into General to do an anaesthetic list once a week commented:

3.21

DR W.: I'm actually quite slow, and I don't actually know who is on the list till I arrive, so I don't usually give pre-meds. So it's necessary to make sure the patients are well asleep before bringing them into theatre, or they [surgeons] will start operating and they're only half asleep.

On the other hand, the anaesthetist will not want to keep the patient unconscious for any longer than necessary, and may attempt to ensure a prompt start to surgery:

3.22
DR J.: The anaesthetist will arrange a pre-med, either directly, or from theatre via the house officer. Timing is critical, so it is essential to be able to predict the length of surgery.

3.23
DR M.: Most people know how long it will take [to prepare the patient], perhaps 30 minutes to an hour for a major case, but some anaesthetists will not start the first case till the surgeon arrives. The surgeon can then go and dictate his letters, we will say, 'We'll call you when we're ready'.

This technique can have its problems however:

3.24
The anaesthetist Dr D. had induced the patient and he was ready for the operation to begin. However the surgeons were in their office. Dr D. went to the scrub room door and shouted, 'Surgeons!' to call them. On a subsequent case, having induced the patient for a very minor procedure, the surgeons were not scrubbed and ready. By the time they were ready, the anaesthetist had been forced to attach monitors because a longer period of unconsciousness was required than originally anticipated.

These criticisms of surgery and surgeons apply to areas considered legitimate concerns for anaesthetists. However, no intimations of incompetence in operating skill itself was ever suggested by an anaesthetist when discussing surgeons: the criticisms were concerned instead with those aspects of a patient's career which were the realm of the anaesthetist, or with apparent surgical inability to act in concert with their anaesthetist partners.

3.25
DR C.: The surgeons regard the theatre as their own, they say what will go on.

3.26
DR F.: Surgeons will only change the way they work if they are forced to by re-organization.

3.27
DR M.: I will see a patient the evening previous to operation, and object

most strongly from the point of view of arranging anaesthesia if subsequently a list is changed.

The data in this section supply a rich vein of material for an analysis of the anaesthetist's discourse. It is grounded in an apparent antipathy to surgeons and all their works. Yet the point from which a deconstruction may begin is signalled in a further comment by an anaesthetist.

3.28
DR J.: An anaesthetist would not acknowledge good surgery any more than vice versa.

The anaesthetist, despite all these criticisms of surgeons, works alongside surgical colleagues, trained in the same biomedical model of disease: yet 'an anaesthetist would not acknowledge good surgery'. It is as if to do so would be to undermine the unity of anaesthetic discourse. This then is something in anaesthetist's discourse which cannot be spoken, and the familiar deconstructive strategy can be performed.

Position: Surgeons are lacking in important skills possessed by anaesthetists.
Negation: Surgeons are skilled in doing resection.
Negation of negation: The skill of a surgeon is something about which to be silent as it constitutes a rival claim to authority.
Deconstruction: Anaesthetists claim that they are the rationalists in the operating theatre in order to downgrade the authority of the surgeon.

The need for anaesthetists to perform such exercises in politics do not require great analysis. As was stated earlier, anaesthetists and surgeons need each other for their work. Anaesthetists have to accept that they are locked into a relationship with surgeons, in which they are usually the underdog. Yet on a daily basis it may be possible to change that balance, in favour of the anaesthetist, while not destroying the wider relationship with surgery without which the scope for anaesthesia would be much reduced. Anaesthetic discourse aims to maximize the opportunities to enhance their authority from day-to-day within the OT, and of course to ensure that in the long term the balance is at least sustained at its current level.

But is this conflict, which is little more than a game of words by which the two groupings sustain their claims to authority, merely the in-fighting power struggle of two specialties? Why is there a need for two specialties anyway – it would seem logical to amalgamate, would it not? The reasons offered for the separation were couched by informants in this study in historical terms, a quirk which particularly in the UK and the USA, led to the separate professional development of anaesthetics as a clinical specialism. The deconstructionist is always wary of such claims to explanation, and would answer that there may have been interesting reasons for this 'quirk' of history. An examination of these possible reasons will occupy the rest of this chapter, beginning with a conversation with informant anaesthetist, Dr J., which was crucial in focusing this investigation of significance of the relationship between anaesthetist and surgeon.

The patient as 'ill' and 'fit'

As part of his moral crusade against the mentality of the surgeon, Dr J. suggested in an interview during the fieldwork that an anaesthetist had a more 'holistic' approach than the surgeon's simple concern with a lesion or dysfunction, and could therefore perceive the patient in her/his full context.

3.29

> DR J.: Assessment for anaesthesia goes hand-in-hand with surgical assessment. Usually an anaesthetist has to do a separate work-up [case-history, examination etc. to assess a patient's condition], because while surgery, and medicine in general is concerned with *disease*, the anaesthetist is concerned with a patient's *fitness*. A patient will be assessed as unfit by an anaesthetist if the disturbance to the system caused by anaesthesia, and aggravated by surgery would threaten survival. That is a different concern to that of the surgeon.
>
> RESEARCHER: Does that affect the questions you ask?
>
> DR J.: Yes, we have to ask questions in relation to health, rather than about the condition to be treated in surgery. [Present author's emphasis]

In this last extract, Dr J. articulates the contrary and in some senses contradictory definitions of the areas of concern of surgeon ('disease') and anaesthetist ('fitness'). This distinction was pursued in subsequent interviews with Dr J. and other anaesthetists and surgeons, and its apparent centrality to understanding the dialogue between the specialties is recognized in this analysis. Although Dr J. made a distinction between 'disease' and 'fitness', following sociological convention (Freidson, 1970, p. 205), it seems acceptable to modify the term 'disease' to 'illness', a concept which incorporates both objective and subjective experience of a deviation from health. His other term – 'fitness' – concerns the patient's capacity to survive and benefit from the surgical procedure, which needs to be addressed by the anaesthetist. The fitness of a patient to undergo surgery seems a most appropriate way of describing the concern of the anaesthetist, in opposition or in dialogue with the surgeon's concern with the patient's illness – the deviation which had led him/her to the surgical setting. The reader will recall that earlier in this chapter this opposition was signalled with regard to the injury caused by surgery to a patient's constitution as a consequence of the removal or reduction in disease.

With these categories in mind it becomes clear that all patients possess both illness and fitness, and that they are *not poles of an opposition, but two separate dimensions*. Only the virtually moribund is entirely ill; all other patients will possess illness and fitness to varying degrees, contingent upon the relative severity of their condition, their personal characteristics and their previous history. The fitness of the patient is a measure of her/his ability to survive the stress of the operation, and is therefore of concern to the anaesthetist, who is designated not only the task of rendering the patient suitable for surgery (unconscious or locally anaesthetized), but also the maintenance of the vital functions during surgery. If s/he is not convinced that these vital functions can be maintained, s/he will declare the patient 'unfit' for surgery.

The conflict with the surgeon's definition of the patient is now clear. The surgeon is interested only in the 'illness' of the patient, her/his deviation from a norm of structure or function. By definition the patient is 'unfit', but in a different sense to that employed by the anaesthetist, for the surgeon, to be ill or unfit is to make a patient suitable for surgery. Surgeon and anaesthetist have different roles in relation to the patient as a result of their particular interests. For the surgeon:

1 The patient presents with a deviation from a norm, an illness.
2 The surgeon alters the illness of the patient, by resection, excision or reconstruction of the deviant tissue.
3 The patient's illness is thereby removed or reduced (if the operation is 'successful').

For the anaesthetist, there is a quite different pattern:

1 The patient presents with a complement of fitness, or capacity to withstand physical stressors.
2 The anaesthetist submits the patient to stressors (surgical shock, anaesthesia) within the limits the patient can tolerate, and monitors the response to ensure these limits are not surpassed.
3 The patient's fitness is thereby (temporarily) removed or reduced.

If this model is correct, an operation represents for the surgeon, the *desirable reduction in illness* of a patient. For the anaesthetist it represents the *undesirable reduction in fitness* of the patient. There is therefore a necessary trade-off of illness and fitness in any operation.

This understanding takes the analysis beyond the earlier deconstruction, suggesting that the opposition between surgeon and anaesthetist derives from their relations to the patient-subject. The discourses which they develop must reflect their positions with regard to the object through which their work is constituted. There must be immanent conflict between the two specialties, for as the surgeon reduces illness, s/he may compromise fitness, and while the anaesthetist conserves fitness, s/he will reduce the opportunities for the surgeon to act effectively. Given that two independent (in the sense of not being poles of a single opposition) dimensions of illness and fitness are involved, the possible outcomes of an operation may be constructed into a 2 × 2 property space as a consequence of this interaction (see Figure 3.1). At first glance, this property space appears to suggest that it is only in the top left-hand quadrant (Cell A) in

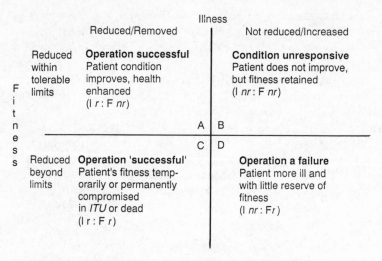

FIGURE 3.1 Interaction of patient illness and fitness. Notation: I = Illness; F = Fitness; r = reduced; nr = not reduced.

which patient outcome will be perceived as successful, in that the deviance is removed or reconstructed, and that the effect of the operation does not itself lead to mortality or further morbidity. In notation, this may be shown as:

$$I\, r : F\, nr > s$$

where I = illness, F = fitness, r = reduced, nr = not reduced, s = success, : = coincident with, and > = results in.

In Cell B, patient fitness is not compromised by the anaesthesia and surgical shock, but the surgical intervention does not resolve the deviance, and may in fact increase the illness. In Cell C, the lesion was successfully resolved, but the compromise to the patient's fitness was very great, although in some cases not permanent or fatal. Surgery on patients in Cell D is unsuccessful, and the effect both of this and of the operation *per se* on fitness leads to deterioration or death.

However, if we inspect the outcomes in these other cells it becomes clear that, by *combining surgical and anaesthetic discourses on the patient*, outcomes in Cells B and C are not necessarily considered as failures. For example, a patient whose outcome is in Cell B (surgery unsuccessful in reducing illness, but anaesthesia successful in retaining stock of fitness) will be perceived as having submitted to the healer, who 'did her/his best', but despite whose efforts did not achieve an improvement; however the patient was not seriously compromised as a consequence. The surgical team will be recognized as acquitting themselves satisfactorily. This outcome may be represented in notation:

$$I\ nr : F\ nr > s$$

Similarly, for patients with an outcome in Cell C, the surgery will be perceived as 'heroic' and the adage 'the operation was a success but the patient died' is applicable, despite the dead or virtually moribund patient at the end of the procedure:

$$I\ r : F\ r > s$$

For both these outcomes, according to the model, the interaction between anaesthetist and surgeon in surgery concerns itself with both illness and fitness, and 'success' is contingent on an unfavourable outcome in respect of both categories. Only in Cell D, where both a *non-reduction in illness and a reduction in fitness* occur together, is the surgical outcome perceived as failure:

$$I\ nr : F\ r > ns$$

Where ns = not success. Only for these patients, who die or are severely weakened by surgery which does not even manage to remove or reconstruct the physical deviance, will approbation not be forthcoming for the surgical team.

This suggests a basis for cooperation between surgeon and anaesthetist, to share a discourse on the patient which can define both their roles as members of the healing profession. While there is always inherent conflict, because surgery may compromise anaesthesia ($I\ r : > F\ r$) or the anaesthetist may refuse to allow high risk surgery ($F\ nr > I\ nr$), there is also the room for cooperation, by which the 'success' of operations can be defined from within discourse in such a way as to vastly increase the likelihood that the outcome can be called 'successful'. Surgeon–anaesthetist cooperation over a patient's illness and fitness permits a wide range of outcomes of surgery to be seen as a passage from an undesirable to a more desirable status. It permits a definition of 'healing' having taken place, even though in a strictly physiological sense some of the procedures may have not achieved any reduction in absolute illness, possibly the reverse.

This analysis seems to have got rather ahead of itself here, extrapolating from fragments of an anaesthetist's discourse to a model with interesting but unproven consequences. So it is necessary to turn back to the ethnography to examine the data. In the next part of this chapter, I will look in detail at further case studies of surgical operations, in terms of the interactions of anaesthetist and surgeon. The case study already examined fits into Cell A of the property space, and I have selected three cases relating to the remaining cells in Figure 3.1 in order to address the predictive capacities of the model in terms of what counts as surgical 'success'.

Before doing so, perhaps it is worth noting a further interesting aspect of the model, concerning the possibility that a patient's outcome might not be fixed, but follows a 'career' through the different cells of the property space. For example, it would follow common-sensically, that a patient initially in Cell C ($Ir : Fr$) may, with the passage of time, and the ministrations of intensive therapy, fully recover from the effects of surgery/anaesthesia and move into cell A. Similarly certain patients initially in Cell D ($I\,nr : F\,r$) may in time move into Cell B, where, despite the persistence of the lesion, no long-term compromise to underlying fitness remains. However, while movements vertically in Figure 3.1 are possible, lateral movements are not possible *without further surgery*. Once illness has been defined as either reduced or not reduced/increased, no subsequent re-definition is possible (or if it is, it cannot be ascribed to surgical intervention). So, while definitions of post-operative illness are permanent, definitions of post-operative fitness can change. What this means, of course, is that normally patient illness will take precedence over patient fitness, because while post-operative illness is defined immediately (so far as the technical success of the resection is concerned), post-operative fitness, although possibly unfavourable to begin with, has uncertainty built into it and may with the passage of time change to a more favourable outcome. It might therefore be predicted that in circumstances of conflict between the two dimensions, projections of favourable post-operative illness will take precedence over coincident projections of post-operative fitness. In other words, the bias will be in favour of operating where there is a chance of reducing illness, despite consequent danger to fitness. There will also be a bias to favour the skills of the surgeon over those of the anaesthetist in terms of their capabilities as 'healers'. This could help to explain the precedence of surgeons over anaesthetists, not only in their claims upon the patient-subject, but in general terms of their authority and prestige within medicine.

Three case studies

The three cases reported below have been selected to look at different combinations of surgeon/anaesthetist interaction (see Figure 3.2). They are real cases,

		Illness	
		High	Low
Fitness — High		**Case 1** Graft	**Case 3** Hypoaesthesia
Fitness — Low		**Case 4** Meningioma	**Case 2** TURP

FIGURE 3.2 Interaction of illness and fitness in four cases.

not amalgams. In two of the cases (2 and 4) there are major complications, in one arising from the anaesthesia and in the other from the surgery. These provide further opportunities to investigate the interaction and assess the extent to which the model predicts what was observed in these cases. In both cases, for reasons which will become clear, details have been slightly altered and disguised.

Case study 2: prostatectomy

Location: General Theatres N
Surgeon: Mr X.
Anaesthetist: Dr Z.
Scrub Nurse: C.
Theatre Sister Y. and one student nurse;
also present ambulance-man trainee, researcher

The patient is an 80-year-old male with a history of angina. The operation is a trans-urethric resection of the prostate (known as TURP), a procedure of removing prostate hypertrophy blocking the urethra by insertion of tubular knives into the urethra from the exterior to cut away the tissue, with electrical diathermy (burning of tissue which seals blood vessels) of the wound.

[3.40 p.m.] The patient was brought to the anaesthetic room in a very drowsy state following pre-med. Dr Z. was to administer a spinal anaesthetic, as the patient was high risk for general anaesthesia. The patient was turned on to his right side and, a local anaesthetic having been applied, the spinal needle was inserted through the skin in between two lumbar vertebrae. Some difficulty was experienced, which the anaesthetist said was because of calcification of the spinal dura which surrounds the spinal cord. The objective in a spinal injection is to enter the sub-arachnoid space, within the outer two meninges (membranes around the cord), but of course taking care not to damage the spinal cord. This requires a learnt skill in order to ensure the correct space has been entered. Once the needle had been positioned correctly, a sterile catheter was introduced via the needle.

3.30

RESEARCHER: How do you know you are in the right space?
DR Z.: You test by feeding in the catheter, if you are in the correct place you
    can easily feed it in.

Dr Z. had some difficulty during this procedure and having not been able to enter the sub-arachnoid space between the vertebrae selected on the first attempt, had to use a second spinal set. Once the tube was in place it was taped to the patient, and a syringe attached by means of which measured doses of anaesthetic could be infused. The patient was taken into theatre and prepared for the operative procedure (lithotomy position, with legs in slings attached to the end of the table), with standard blood pressure and heart rate monitors. The induction had taken 30 minutes.

Mr X. began the procedure, which in normal circumstances is considered relatively minor. The anaesthetic agent was infused at a given rate calculated from the patient's weight. Although stupefied by the pre-med, it soon became apparent that the patient was still experiencing some sensation. Some 15 minutes into the procedure there was the following exchange

3.31

MR X.: It's no good whenever I use the diathermy he moves. [The implication is that there is poor analgesia]
DR Z.: Well I have given the patient all the anaesthetic which he can safely receive.
MR X.: I cannot carry on with the procedure when he is moving.
DR Z.: I don't think the spinal is working. I had better put him under.

Dr Z. had introduced the entire dose of spinal anaesthetic according to his calculations of safety, but it had become clear that the spinal needle had failed to penetrate into the sub-arachnoid space, and consequently the anaesthetic had no direct effect on blocking sensation from the area of the operation. It was now too late to attempt a new spinal, so Dr Z. had no choice but to induce the patient, who is still affected by the pre-med, into general anaesthesia using a gaseous agent. The operation was concluded satisfactorily with the patient unconscious. The procedure ended, and the patient awakened, Dr Z. spent some time in the recovery area to ensure that he was comfortable.

In this case study, the anaesthetist has been forced to compromise the patient's fitness by a general anaesthetic, which the patient's age and history made high risk, because the spinal had not worked (probably because it was not in the correct space inside the meninges). A minor surgical procedure (low or medium illness) was transformed from having little effect on fitness to having a greater effect. Patient outcome, which should have been in Cell A ($I\,r : F\,nr > s$) was forced into Cell C ($I\,r : F\,r > s$).

There was an alternative, that of abandoning surgery halfway through. This could have led to an outcome in Cell B ($I\,nr : F\,nr > s$), but there was always a danger that it could have ended in Cell D ($I\,nr : F\,r > ns$) given the effect on this frail patient of the unfinished surgery and the lack of analgesia. In the circumstances, the anaesthetist had no choice but to acquiesce, and administer general anaesthesia. The consequence was that the anaesthetist was unable to fulfil his role of proxy for the patient's fitness during the operation, and the conflict thus generated led to a very poor outcome for the patient, compared to what might normally be expected for this procedure. Significant pressure was placed upon an anaesthetist by a surgeon to act in a way which compromised the patient's fitness against the original judgement of what was appropriate in the case of this old man. The outcome, however, from the clinician's point of view, was that healing had taken place, that the operation was a 'success'. There would be an expectation that a Cell C outcome would, with careful therapy, become a Cell A outcome in due course.

In the next case study, the anaesthetist conducted complex procedures to ensure the patient's fitness was not compromised during what was a very minor procedure.

Case study 3: hypoaesthesia of thumb

Location: Plastic Theatres
Surgeon: Mr T.
Anaesthetist: Dr B.
Scrub Nurse D.; also present Nurse C., anaesthetic nurse J., two surgical registrars, researcher

The patient was a 20-year-old male with hypoaesthesia (lack of sensation) in the distal joint of his right thumb following an accident. The procedure to be undertaken was the micro-surgical dissection of the thumb to expose a severed nerve. The ends of this nerve would be opposed to encourage healing and the recovery of sensation. The patient has been admitted on a day basis.

[11 a.m.] The patient was pre-medicated in the anaesthetic room of plastic theatres by Dr B. The surgical procedure was intricate but minor, taking some 30 minutes. However a degree of post-operative pain was to be expected due to the operation being on a nerve, and the anaesthetic to be employed was therefore a brachial block. This supplied analgesia far more effectively than local anaesthetic – a general anaesthetic being inappropriate for this minor procedure.

3.32

RESEARCHER: Why not use a local anaesthetic?
DR B.: A block is more elegant, you are affecting the nerve at a higher level, and the result will be better pain control. It is harder to administer, it is a mixture of experience and guesswork where the nerve plexus is, and you do not want to inject actually into a nerve.

As he was administering the injection, to the upper arm just below the armpit, apparently with considerable discomfort to the patient, Dr B. explained that blocks were also unpredictable in how long they took to act – the norm being 20 minutes. The patient was left in the anaesthetic room for the block to take effect. No numbness had resulted after 30 minutes, and with the surgeons impatient to begin and the patient now sleepy with the pre-med, he is taken into theatre and preparations begun, despite there not yet being analgesia in the affected part. After a further 10 minutes the absurd spectacle was presented of Dr B. quietly approaching the drowsy patient and jabbing his finger with a sterile needle. The patient jumped and commented, 'What was that?' to a retreating Dr B. After a further wait, repetition of the needle prick without this response indicated that the block had taken effect and surgery was able to begin. The surgery itself was uneventful, the surgeon using microscopy to dissect down to the nerve and oppose the ends. An intricate dressing which would immobilize the damaged thumb was instigated under the supervision of the surgeon, and amid joking about the inability of the patient (a student) to write his examinations as a consequence. This completed, the patient was dispatched to the recovery area, from which, in due course, he was discharged. As will be seen in Chapter 4, discharge is one way in which a label of 'healed' is attached to a patient.

In this case study, while the surgery itself was highly skilled, the emphasis was on the preparations to ensure that the procedure was pain free. Thus a minor degree of illness was successfully treated with patient outcome in Cell A (I r : F $nr > s$). If the patient had suffered a large amount of post-operative pain (reduction in fitness) with such a procedure, the outcome could have been perceived as being in Cell C. Given that there was no guarantee of the healing of the nerve and restoration of sensation, the possibility of a Cell D outcome (I nr : F $r > ns$) might even have been possible. Consequently there was an emphasis on the process of anaesthesia, which in fact took longer than the surgery itself – a circumstance common in plastic-surgery theatres. In one case observed, anaesthesia using a femoral block took 30 minutes for a five-minute surgical procedure on a patient's leg. The apparent trivial nature of plastic theatres surgery may have led to the need for the following conversation:

3.33
SENIOR REGISTRAR SURGEON O.: Are you interested in plastic surgery?
RESEARCHER: Well I am visiting all the theatres to see the range of surgery.
O.: Plastic surgery is interesting; it's the only kind of surgery which reconstructs as well as resects.

Anaesthetists were observed to have a great deal of autonomy in plastic theatres at General, and the layout of the OT, with its anaesthetic rooms separated from theatre by a corridor (see Figure 2.2 on p. 18), may serve to enhance this autonomy. During the period of field work, surgeons were never observed to enter plastic anaesthetic rooms. The complex anaesthetic procedures were taken very seriously, in contrast to the very relaxed atmosphere in the operating theatre, the only one where desultory conversation and joking were regular features. Visitors would appear in street clothes at the door of the theatre, and chat to whoever they had come to see with little concern for the routines observed in other theatres. On the other hand, the anaesthetic room was virtually

SURGEONS AND ANAESTHETISTS   71

sacrosanct when occupied by a patient. The last case study indicates the significance of this reversal – in plastic theatres, the 'success' of the operation is far more contingent on anaesthetists' conservation of fitness than in other more major surgery, where there is greater scope for the resolution of illness. Indeed, the surgeon is unable to influence the discourse of healing to the extent to which the anaesthetist is able in these forms of minor surgery.

The last case is the most complex. It describes an operation which is clearly categorized as unsuccessful, in Cell D, although as will be seen it is rescued at the last minute from disaster, and reconstituted into another cell.

Case study 4: Meningioma

Location: Neuro-theatres
Surgeon: Mr C.; senior registrar and two surgical house doctors
Anaesthetists: Dr A. and two registrars
Scrub nurse Sister A.; three nurses: also present researcher, visitor

Patient was a 63-year-old female with a tumour of the meninge covering the cerebral cortex requiring excision to relieve a life-threatening pressure on the brain.

[11 a.m.] The patient, who had been admitted as an urgent case, was brought to the anaesthetic room, which is an annexe of neuro-theatre B (see Figure 2.3 on p. 19). Before her arrival, Dr A. and Mr C. viewed brain scans indicating the position of the tumour and discussed the patient's history – there is no contraindication for general anaesthesia although the patient is poorly as a result of her condition. Induction was by standard infusion into left forefinger cannula, and administration of gaseous agent. Once unconscious the patient was transferred from the trolley to the operating table, which in neuro-theatres is mobile, enabling it to be brought into the anaesthetic room. With the patient anaesthetized and receiving gaseous agent, the patient's head was clamped with an attachment connected to the end of the table which tightens metal points through the scalp into the skull, under the direct supervision of Mr C. Leads for blood pressure, heart rate, electrocardiograph (ECG) and electroencephalograph (EEG) were connected to the patient's head, chest and limbs. The patient was draped and the table wheeled into the theatre.

In neurosurgery, the head is necessarily the preserve of the surgeon, while the tubes supplying gaseous agents and monitoring leads are fed under the drapes, down towards the patient's feet, and thence to the anaesthetic trolley. The anaesthetist and assistants take up position next to this trolley, and their attention is mainly devoted to observing the range of monitors. With two registrars, there is an abundance of anaesthetic support, enabling Dr A. regularly to visit an earlier patient in recovery, and perform other tasks in the anaesthetic room. The patient was draped so only a small piece of scalp remained exposed. As a flap of scalp was incised, clamps were attached by the assisting surgeon to the cut edges to prevent bleeding from this highly vascularized skin. The skull was then trephinned with three burr holes, sawn through and a section removed to provide access to the tumour. The meninges thus exposed were opened to reveal the surface of the brain and the tumour. The operation to remove the tumour was relatively quick, with the tumour provisionally identified as a meningioma, excised, and sent for biopsy. Although meningiomas are usually benign, they are highly vascular, and there was considerable haemorrhage after excision. When this had been stemmed, the meninges were sutured, the skull replaced and glued in place with the shavings of bone saved from the earlier sawing, and the scalp sutured. The procedure was completed by 12.30 p.m., and with surgery completed, the patient was brought to consciousness. Patients undergoing neurosurgery were not expected to provide the extent of response (speak a few words, grimace) expected of other patients. A hospital bed was brought from the recovery area directly into theatre, and supervised by Mr C., the patient was transferred directly to this, removing the need for an intermediate transfer to a trolley. The bed was wheeled by the anaesthetists, via the anaesthetic room to the recovery area, which is fully equipped for intensive therapy at 1.10 p.m.

Thus far, the case study suggests far less autonomy for the anaesthetist than in other theatres. The surgeon enters the anaesthetic room, discusses aspects of the surgery which may influence choice of anaesthetic agent, supervises the positioning of the patient on the table and draping. The fitness of the patient is secondary to her illness, as a consequence of the severity of the condition. Compromise to fitness is seen as an essential and necessary trade-off against reduction in illness, which if untreated would quickly kill the patient. It is the surgeon who defines the course of the operation, and the anaesthetist accepts her/his authority. A claim to anaesthetic authority which might prevent surgery being conducted on the grounds of the lack of fitness of the patient would be unjustifiable. The success of the operation requires a removal of disease, and within the context of the heroic procedures of neurosurgery, reductions in fitness are an accepted risk. If the risks were judged too great, the neurosurgeon would do nothing apart from standing by and watching the patients deteriorate or die: an unlikely position from which to achieve authority!

3.34

SURGEON MR C.: We do not really have a concept of elective surgery in neuro. Most of the patients we see in out-patients are admitted as urgent cases, in that if they are not operated on their condition will deteriorate. There is no choice but surgery in most cases.

The balance between fitness and illness is pushed to the extreme in neurosurgery, the opposite extreme to the plastic surgery of Case 3.

In the case of the meningioma patient, so far the outcome of the surgery might be expected to be Cell C ($Ir : Fr > s$). However, in this case study, the outcome was not as expected. At 2.40 p.m., Mr C. was operating to excise a benign tumour from the third ventricle of another patient's brain. The anaesthetist Dr A. was summoned to the recovery room to look at the former patient by the recovery nurse: her EEG trace indicated unconsciousness as opposed to sleep. After conducting some tests, Mr A. returned to theatre:

3.35

DR A.: Mrs X. seems to be a bit flat. She's displaying a ―― [some technical detail of brain wave pattern – not caught]. I wonder if you would like to have a look.

MR C.: She's unconscious? [*Dr A. assents*] Yes I'll come in. [*He quickly leaves theatre for recovery, his assistant continuing the operation.*]

Dr A. had diagnosed a sub-arachnoid haemorrhage, resulting in a blood clot which was causing pressure on the brain, and thus the lapse into unconsciousness. Without emergency surgery, the patient would rapidly deteriorate. Leaving the recovery area, Mr C. quickly arranged with the theatre sister for the third neuro-theatre – which earlier that day he had told the researcher was non-commissionable because of cutbacks – to be opened to receive the patient. Returning to his current patient, his assistant (senior registrar) was delegated to conduct the emergency procedure consisting of re-opening the skull and meninges, removing the clot, determining and resolving the source of the haemorrhage. A house officer assisted, Dr A. administered the anaesthesia, and nurses from theatre B serviced the emergency. [3.20 p.m.] The tiny theatre was packed as other personnel including a consultant surgeon from neuro-theatre A and other staff filtered in to watch the drama.

Back in theatre B, surgery continued but things were suddenly very quiet, with only Mr C., a registrar anaesthetist, a scrub nurse and the researcher, who was called into service to move or adjust equipment in the absence of a circulating nurse. By 4 p.m. this operation had been completed, and the patient taken to recovery. Mr C. slipped into theatre C to watch the emergency operation, which had progressed to the painstaking removal of the clotted blood which had haemorrhaged from the site of the operation earlier in the day.

It was immediately obvious that some kind of reversal of roles had occurred. The anaesthetist, who had accepted the surgical definition of patients in the routine list, now had authority. With the pressure of the clot removed, the patient had a better prognosis, but there had been considerable shock to the patient's system, and Dr A. was concerned about a low blood pressure and a weak ECG trace. The surgeon, a senior registrar and Dr A.'s junior, carried out the surgery needed to preserve the patient, while two consultant surgeons looked on. Mr C. watched from just inside the door, no longer claiming any rights over his former patient. By 5.45 p.m. the emergency operation was completed and the patient taken to recovery from whence she would be moved to the ITU in a very poorly condition.

In this last case study, the outcome turns out to be far from certain. In terms of the model it would be in Cell C

$$I\,r:F\,r>s$$

with the reasonable expectation of movement to Cell A in due course. But the subsequent developments suggested outcome in Cell D:

$$I\,nr:F\,r>ns$$

in which not only has the surgery failed to reduce the patient's illness, but the consequence of it upon the patient's fitness has been catastrophic. This outcome cannot be perceived as a success.

What happened subsequently overturns all the expectations of the hierarchy of neurosurgery. Dr A., an anaesthetist, took control. Under his guidance, an operation was conducted with the simple objective of restoring fitness compromised by an earlier unsuccessful piece of surgery. Mr C. had not only reduced a patient's fitness, but also failed to complete the removal of illness. He alone, within the discourse of neurosurgery which permitted him to take so much authority for the conduct of the operation, had failed. It is open to Dr A., within an anaesthetic discourse which is more suited to other forms of surgery, to claim the authority to direct the rescue. And after this second operation, which resolved the haemorrhage, the patient not only had her illness reduced (the completion of the excision of the tumour) but her fitness was restored to at least a level which might eventually recover given appropriate therapy. An outcome in Cell C, a 'success' snatched from the jaws of failure by the intervention of an anaesthetist with his claim to authority grounded in a commitment to patient fitness.

Discussion

The four case studies of operations in this chapter represent the four interactions of surgeon and anaesthetist in a 2×2 property space of outcomes of fitness and illness, variables which should not be seen as opposites, but as separate dimensions. Fitness constitutes the anaesthetic discourse on the patient, while it is through a discourse on illness that surgeons constitute their subject. Of course, for the surgeon, the opposite of the concept of illness will be 'health' or some such, with a strength of constitution being part of this. For the anaesthetist, the opposing pole to fitness will be some idea of absence of resilience, and no doubt any illness a patient possesses will be part of this. These negations of the positive poles of the dimensions are themselves negated in constituting the respective discourses of the two specialties.

The reader will by now be sufficiently versed in the methodology of deconstruction to see how each of these discourses can be analysed, and in particular how such deconstruction explains the depth of antagonism between specialties, and how locally constituted discourses serve the interests of the two specialties. As with all deconstruction, the irony which is exposed is that it is the pole of the opposition which is negated which defines the possibility of action. For the anaesthetist, it is the lack of fitness (including illness) which makes a patient's fitness something which is to be conserved, while for the surgeon, the possession of a reserve of health makes the patient's illness something which there is value in reducing.

So these antagonisms – constituted through the negations of the specialties perspective on their patient – have a significance only in the context of the necessary symbiosis of the specialties. The anaesthetist's single-minded discursive commitment to fitness is significant *only* in relation to surgery; the surgeon's concern with illness, to the exclusion of all other parts of a patient, is possible only in relation to anaesthetics. The two specialties constitute their subjects as if theirs were the only possible discourse, yet may do so only in relation to each other. Where one specialty has little room to flex its authority (surgeons in plastic, anaesthetists in neurosurgery), the other *must* do so in order for both to sustain the logic of an underlying shared discourse. In these situations one specialty acquiesces, and the discourse of the other specialty carries more weight, to sustain both in the common enterprise of surgical healing.

The discourse on surgical healing is thus articulated by the combination of fitness/illness outcome, mediated via the specialties of surgery and anaesthetics. The model developed in this chapter suggests that the discourse on surgical healing copes with three out of the four combinations of illness/fitness outcome: only the worst case causes a problem of definition of the post-operative patient. Having recognized the symbiosis of surgeon and anaesthetist, whose respective discourses on their patients mediate their respective technical activities in the OT, allows this analysis of surgical healing to progress through a further act of deconstruction. The polarity which informs the shared discourse of surgeon and anaesthetist is around the paradox that surgery can heal only by injury.

Position: Surgery acts to enhance the well-being of the patient.
Negation: Surgery injures a patient.
Negation of negation: The injury to a patient is a temporary loss of fitness, of little importance in relation to the long-term advantage of undergoing surgery.
Deconstruction: The effects of surgery upon a patient are ignored in the claim that it heals.

This deconstruction offers an understanding of something recognized by Parsons (1951) in his functionalist reading of the roles of doctor and patient. He noted that the doctor is legitimated in injuring the patient during treatment, and that this will not be a source of blame to be attributed to a doctor, so long as it is well-intended. The Parsonian 'explanation' is not really an explanation – it is that this legitimacy is functional for bringing a deviant sick person back into normal society. My reading is quite different in that it begins with the paradoxical nature of what is called 'healing'. It then shows how this is manipulated by those who do the clinical interventions through discourse, in such a way that it will constitute what is done as healing rather than actual bodily harm, and themselves as healers, with all the authority and status which goes with that title.

In the case of surgery, the symbiosis of surgeon and anaesthetist contributes additional elements to this manipulation. The complexities of two opposing discourses which have been examined in this chapter serve to enhance the extent to which a positive outcome can be claimed. All medical treatment is more or less uncomfortable or painful, and so the paradox exists in every specialty. It is tempting to suggest that while other specialties have to grin and bear the paradox, surgery, in its utilization of the technique of anaesthesia, has found a way which allows a range of outcomes to be seen as successes which in any other sphere of medicine would be considered disastrous in the effect that treatment has on a patient, dramatically increasing pain, reducing mobility, and possibly threatening life itself. Before anaesthetics, surgery was feared, and the surgeon was seen as little better than a butcher. Anaesthesia brought its own risks to life, but enabled far more surgery and more extensive surgery to be performed, in cases where the threat of disease to life outweighed the dangers of the surgery itself. Today, six-day post-operative deaths account for 5.3 per 1000 operations, with only one-tenth of this figure attributable to the anaesthesia itself (Lunn and Mushin, 1982). The symbiosis of the specialties has meant that less than 1 operation in 2000 is thus an outright 'failure' in terms of the discourses which have been outlined in the preceding pages. The effect on surgical authority and prestige might be expected to reflect these rates.

This discussion has brought the study to a point at which the relations between the techniques of surgery and the power of the specialty have been fundamentally articulated. The deconstruction has placed the paradox of surgery as disease remover and patient injurer at this focus. In Chapter 4, the proposition will be examined using further data from the ethnography, this time looking at the ways surgeons interact with their patients on the wards, the things they say, and the discourses which they use to constitute what they do.

4

SURGEONS ON THE WARDS

Introduction

In this chapter the study turns to a further aspect of the ethnographic material gathered during fieldwork at General Hospital, to look at the interactions between surgeons and their patients and with other staff which occur when they visit the surgical wards. For the first time in this book patients get in on the ethnography in a conscious state, rather than as the silent, sleeping or heavily doped individuals around which surgery revolves, unable to offer their own version of events. Unlike these silent bodies, conscious human agents clearly have a potential to influence surgical discourse, and this chapter is devoted to addressing the extent of that influence. Tuckett (1985) has suggested that we can understand the interactions between doctor and patient as a 'meeting between experts' – both parties possessing authoritative discourses upon the patient's body, one by dint of ownership, the other through professional status. So when patients are conscious, surgeons are no longer the only 'expert' present, and to sustain their authority they will have to deal with possibly contrary definitions of what surgery is about, how patients are to be categorized, and the extent of surgical 'success'. The focus of the chapter is therefore the ways surgeons use these interactions with their patients to their advantage in constituting their (surgeons') perspective on surgical healing.

Surgical ward rounds can be very rapid affairs. Some consultant surgeons, having seen the patient at an out-patient clinic, leave pre-operative admission entirely to their junior staff and may not see their patients pre-operatively, until they appear unconscious in theatre. Others conduct a round, and these pre-operative rounds are the quickest. On one occasion during fieldwork, a surgeon who was fairly lukewarm about having a sociologist on ward rounds began a pre-operative round five minutes early, so that having arrived at the appointed hour, I learnt that the round had already been completed. Some surgeons visit their patients the evening after they have undergone surgery, when they have been moved from the recovery room to their ward or to the Intensive Therapy Unit. These are also brief, the patients usually being still very drowsy or asleep as an after-effect of the anaesthetic, or of post-operative analgesia; the round primarily consists of a short report from the junior staff of the surgical firm on each patient's physiological status post-operatively.

Subsequent post-operative rounds are more leisurely, as the patient is usually capable of some interaction. In addition, rounds are highly routinized opportunities for the members of the surgical firm to meet and discuss the patients currently in their care, an opportunity for the medical and nursing staff to negotiate over the patients' surgical careers. As will be seen from some of the extracts of interactions reported in the coming pages, these opportunities sometimes have the authority of the consultant as the topic. For all these reasons, analysis of ward round interaction should assist in understanding the social processes by which surgical healing is achieved. Observation of ward round interactions suggests that they can be understood in terms of three themes:

Theme 1 The physiological condition of the patient, as judged by staff from clinical tests, physical examination for clinical signs and enquiry to the patient as to her/his subjective experience.

Theme 2 The condition of the surgical wound and its dressing.

Theme 3 Prognosis – the extent to which the condition for which surgery was undertaken has been resolved, the stage to which a patient is making a recovery, and upon a projected discharge date from the hospital ward.

As will be seen in this chapter, all these themes are surgeon-centred, the first is the most surgeon-centred, relying heavily on technical analysis. The third is the least, involving the possibility of patients having some influence on the decisions reached.

The ward round is a highly structured organizational form which enables surgeons to set the agenda for the interaction. In the extreme case a patient may not be included directly in the round at all, except to receive a greeting from the consultant and a brief resume of the clinical assessment before the round moves on. This is rare in post-operative rounds as patients tend to make progress quickly on surgical wards, and so judgements of condition have to be made on each ward round. From time to time, a more articulate patient may gain temporary access to this agenda, sometimes with the cooperation of the surgeon, and occasionally without it, as will be seen. However, the usual course of these interactions is very tightly controlled by the surgeon, and has the effect of defining and categorizing patients according to criteria which surgeons set out. Unlike the situation in theatre, where as described in Chapter 3 alternative definitions of patients by anaesthetists can affect the activities which surgeons can undertake, on the wards there is only the patient to offer an alternative, and of course, the patient is in a vulnerable position relative to the surgeon. I shall seek to demonstrate in this chapter how these categorizations emphasize the significance of the surgical operation in the patient's sickness 'career'.

Theme 1: the discourse on patient physiology

The interactions which take place on the ward round may be separated into those conducted between staff members and those between surgeon and patient. Usually the consultant surgeon spends some time in discussion with the junior surgical staff prior to any interaction with the patient, in order to familiarize her/himself with recent developments.

4.1

The 4 p.m. ward round began on the male surgical ward, with the arrival of the consultant Mr D. A registrar and the house officer were waiting at the end of the ward. With myself as the most junior member of the round we processed up the centre of the ward to the nursing station, where the staff nurse was waiting with the trolley containing the files on the patients in the ward. The registrar supplied the consultant with information on one patient whose progress was of concern, then we moved to the first patient on the round. The nurse supplied the relevant file, and the three doctors then discussed the patient for some moments, Mr D. referring to the notes and to the chart at the bottom of the bed. Only after this did Mr D. greet the patient by name.

After any direct interaction with the patient, which as will be seen entails verbal commentary or discussion, plus physical examination if appropriate, there will usually be a further period of inter-staff discussion. In both these periods, much of the discussion concerns the patient's physiological condition, and will involve reports of tests, monitoring of outputs and proposals for further tests or medication. These tests are all problem-oriented: they define the patient in terms of her/his forthcoming operation, or her/his response to it:

4.2

Patient H. had been admitted for repair of inguinal hernia and fistula, and his GP had written to say that because of a history of ischaemic heart disease, H. was not suited to general anaesthesia. However this information contradicted the opinion of a surgical consultant who had assessed H. as suitable for general anaesthetic on the occasion of an operation four years previously. To square this contradiction, tests were being carried out on H. in order to make a decision about the form of anaesthesia to be adopted. It thus appeared inappropriate to devote more than the briefest moments with the patient, as no decision had been reached. The consultant and junior staff discussed the possibilities for some time, standing some feet from the end of H's bed. The preference of the consultant was for a general if possible.

Occasionally, these discussions on physiology spill over into the surgeon–patient interaction during the round:

4.3

[*Patient B. had had surgery to remove a tumour of the gastro-intestinal tract. During surgery, the tumour had been found to be disseminated, and during the operation B. had had a cardiac arrest. B. was conscious but poorly.*]

MR D.: [to junior staff and researcher]: Despite what we've done he seems to be getting better. How is his —— [*a long discussion on technical details of the patients metabolism ensues, including reports on tests and suggestions of further tests and action to stabilize the patient's condition*]. [*The house doctor introduces the problem of the surgical wound, which was leaking as a consequence of having been very rapidly closed following the cardiac arrest on the operating table. The discussion now focuses upon this problem, and the relative advantages of different forms of skin sutures and staples were debated among the staff. After about five minutes Mr D. addresses the patient.*]

MR D.: How are you Mr B.? Are you feeling less sick now?

PATIENT B.: Yes, less sick.

The interaction with the patient in this extract appears to be an afterthought, but in fact it continues the theme of the physiology of the patient, whose self-report of his condition is used to make a decision concerning future management of the case. The discourse does not develop into a more patient-centred theme with an emphasis on recovery (Theme 3). In the case of patient B., the nature of his condition (an advanced malignancy) may have precluded this deviation. In other patients, however, where there is a more positive evaluation of potential outcome and recovery (Theme 3), especially on the part of the patient, a discourse on physiology initiated by the surgeon can lead to conflict of interpretation. In the following case, an inter-staff discussion of a patient's physiology concerning lack of bowel function as a result of a road traffic accident is continued in the first exchanges of surgeon–patient interaction:

4.4

MR D.: Hello, Miss F. [*sits on edge of bed*] Have you passed any wind yet? [*Because he is a gastro-intestinal (GI) surgeon, Mr D. has an interest in post-operative flatulence as a clinical sign of GI function.*]

PATIENT F.: No. Can I take this [oxygen] mask off?

NURSE [*sharply*]: No, not yet.

MR D.: You can take the mask off when you can breath, when the bruising on your lungs has gone down. We are going to give you a couple of suppositories which will get you unblocked, because your bowels are bruised too; that will reduce the swelling here, and that'll make your breathing easier. [*To researcher*] I said she was going to be a difficult patient.

Here the patient has subverted the discourse on physiology into one on recovery. Interestingly, Mr D's usual way of asking about post-operative flatulence is more folksy: 'Have you passed any wind out of your tail-end yet?' The question thus framed offers a more patient-centred interpretation, and it is usually concerned with Theme 3 (recovery/discharge). In the case of Patient F., who was admitted with a silent abdomen, the wording was not intended to indicate a significance other than within the surgeon-centred discourse on physiology. The subverting of the discourse away from the surgeon's discourse, necessitating a long explanation in terms of Theme 3, is demonstrated by the comment to the researcher at the end.

The discourse on physiology is a surgeon-orientated technique for categorizing the pre- or post-operative patient. Pre-operatively, the patient's physiology is a sign which determines the patient as a suitable case for surgical treatment. It will consist of the whole gamut of symptoms and clinical signs, plus possible investigations or biopsies conducted in the pre-operative period. All these have the purpose of categorizing the patient as a surgical case, and once the categorization has been made, then future activity is clear and unquestionable. If the discourse on physiology does not confirm that right, interest in a patient is quickly lost, as in the case of patient P., who was originally admitted for a cholecystectomy, but after tests is now to be transferred to a medical ward, to be treated non-surgically:

4.5

[*There is a very brief discussion at the foot of the bed, during which the transfer to a medical ward is confirmed by the house doctor.*]

MR D.: [*addresses patient*]: How are you today?

PATIENT P.: Not too bad.

MR D.: We're just waiting for Dr X. [medical consultant] to fix you up. It'll be Thursday [the next day], or maybe Friday. Then you'll be all sorted out. Goodbye.

Mr D. has already started to move on to the next patient. The house doctor comments that the medical procedure is in fact arranged for the Friday. Mr D. replies in a disinterested tone, 'Friday, is it?'

When there is no such difficulty in categorizing a patient as suitable for surgery, the discourse on physiology, being a surgeon-centred discourse, should ensure that the progress towards surgery moves inexorably. In the following extract from a pre-operative discussion between a female gynaecology consultant surgeon and her senior registrar Dr S., the consultant seemed concerned that the discourse might be subverted:

4.6

MRS A.: Where is Dr S. [registrar]?

STAFF NURSE: He's looking at patient X.

MRS A.: He's taking his time, that fistula need not take him so long. Ten minutes, that's a long internal examination.[1]

DR S. [*arriving at the staff group*]: It's just a small hole in the rear wall.

MRS A.: Will you do it tomorrow afternoon?

DR S.: Yes, I'll try.

MRS A.: In that case put it down for me, and I will do it myself. [2]

DR S.: No, I can do . . .

MRS A.: . . . It's just that word 'try' that I do not like, Dr S. I don't like it at all.

MRS A.: [Later *to researcher*] I do not like Dr S., he is rude to the patients. The trouble with Dr S. is that he cannot speak the Queen's English. [3]

Patient X's fistula has the effect of categorizing her as a suitable case for surgery, and Dr S's painstaking examination seems to Mrs A. unnecessary, interrupting a discourse in which there is an 'obvious' need for surgical intervention. Mrs A. resists any such interruption by firstly imputing sexual misconduct to Dr S. [1], threatening to deny Dr S's access to the patient [2] and commenting on his ethnic background (in fact the same as Mrs A's, but from an inferior caste) [3]. By these techniques, Dr S's deviation from the script does not sully Mrs A's own right as surgeon to conduct surgery.

Post-operatively, the discourse on physiology is similarly concerned with guaranteeing the surgeon's right to have intervened to heal the patient. In this extract, a patient is being told what has been done during the operation, but the conversation develops into a series of re-definitions of the patient:

4.7

MRS A.: Hello, Miss E., we sorted everything out for you; we've taken the [fallopian] tube, but the ovary is still there as usual.

PATIENT E.: You left the ovary?

MRS A.: Oh yes, we *never* take the ovary. [1] So everything's fine [2]; but come and see us when you are trying for a baby, as you only have one tube now . . .

PATIENT E.: I don't want a baby.

MRS A.: [*to nurse*]: Fix her up with contraceptives, the sheath. [3]

MISS E.: I thought I'd use an IUD.

MRS A.: No, I don't want you on IUD or mini-pill; use the sheath and foam. [4]

The surgeon first confirmed that despite having removed a fallopian tube, by leaving the ovary intact she had not interfered with the patient's normal female hormonal balance, and thus her femininity (this was emphasized by Mrs A. to the researcher as of great importance during a number of similar operations), and goes on to say that she is 'fine' [1, 2]. A second re-definition occurs when Mrs A. suggested that Miss E. will fulfil the role of mother in due course. When the patient denied this desire, the surgeon turned away from her, and spoke about her in the third person to the nurse, commenting on a need for future sexual regulation [3]. Finally there was a return to the discourse on physiology with a comment which referred to the patient's new status as a person with an impaired reproductive system which could be affected by contraception [4].

This re-definition of patients is a significant feature of the discourse of physiology when used post-operatively, and hence this theme is extremely valuable in evaluating the success of surgery. However, sometimes the theme is unsatisfactory, and in these circumstances re-definition is not possible. Mrs O., a very old patient who has had a cardiac arrest on the operating table, does not offer the surgeon the usual rights to categorization via the discourse on physiology:

4.8

[*Mrs O. was a very small woman virtually obscured by a mass of high-technology equipment placed around her bed: monitors, a complicated three-way drip and ECG equipment, all of which had been erected post-operatively by the medical (as opposed to surgical) staff, who had become involved following the arrest. Mr D. stopped some way back from the end of the bed with his junior colleagues.*]

MR D.: That's a very impressive array of tackle. [*The word 'tackle' is used derisively, and the others smile.*]

[*Mr D. approaches the patient who mutters unintelligibly.*]

MR D.: You're doing fine.

MRS O.: Nnnnnnnnn . . .

[*Mr D. holds her hand and tries to make eye contact beneath the oxygen mask. When there is no response, he turns to the equipment, and after looking it over starts to fiddle with one of the taps attached to the drip. After a few seconds he turns away.*]

MR D.: [*to house doctor*]: Here's a bit of IT [intensive therapy] for you.

HOUSE DOCTOR: I'm enjoying it.

Here the equipment represents an unsatisfactory discourse on the patient's physiology, firstly because it was erected by non-surgical staff, and the patient is now no longer a surgical problem, her main sickness now being a consequence of the cardiac arrest. Nor does the patient respond to Mr D's bedside manner, which would enable an alternative discourse to be invoked. Consequently Mrs O's continued presence on the surgical ward is anomalous, she is 'matter out of place' to use Douglas's (1984) term, and Mr D's last comment suggests that the Intensive Therapy Unit (ITU) is the right place for her, rather than his ward.

When patients intervene in the discourse on physiology, the possibility is that the theme is subverted in a way which is unsatisfactory from the surgeon's point of view.

4.9

[*Mrs F. had had an ectopic pregnancy, and had a fallopian tube removed as a consequence.*]

PATIENT F.: I have a list of questions which I wrote down, because I was a bit hazy when you explained before the operation. [*Surgeon Mrs A. nods*] What exactly have you taken?

MRS A.: We have taken the right tube, that's all.

PATIENT F.: Not the ovary?

MRS A.: We never take the ovary, so you have two good ovaries.

PATIENT F.: So will this make it difficult for me to conceive? [1]

MRS A.: No you can produce an egg every month, same as before.

PATIENT F.: But I will only have a chance every other month? [2]

MRS A.: No, just the same, you have both ovaries.

PATIENT F.: But one is not connected to anything . . . [3]

MRS A.: No we can't just say which one will produce an egg each month. [4]

In this sequence, the questions at points [1], [2] and [3] force the surgeon to admit that the operation has not returned the patient to the status of 'normal' fertility, and is forced at [4] to fall back on the randomness of ovulation as a response, thereby at least avoiding being allocated the moral status as potential scapegoat for a future infertility. At this point, Mrs A. hurriedly departed, preventing any further questions.

By the nature of the major surgery carried out by some surgeons, a number of their patients end up in the Intensive Therapy Unit following their operations. In ITU the physiology of the patient becomes the concern of the ITU nursing staff and anaesthetists. Ward rounds include post-operative visits to the ITU when a consultant has a patient there. The discourse on physiology is unsatisfactory in these circumstances, and interactions down-play the involvement of the surgeon in care, substituting a kind of empathic mood.

4.10

After rounds in the male and female wards, there was a visit to Intensive Therapy to see patient J., who had haemorrhaged during an operation to excise a tumour in the abdomen, and had barely survived. The visit consisted principally of a discussion between Mr D. and the duty anaesthetist on the patient's physiological condition, which was giving extreme cause for concern. Mr D. then turned to patient J. and offered a few words of encouragement to the patient. The latter appeared extremely frightened by his circumstances, and responded by gripping Mr D's hand. Mr D. seemed to derive comfort from this. On leaving the ITU he was subdued. He asked the researcher, 'Have you ever been in one of these places before? Just think what it's like for J'. The ward round ended on a sombre note, with the inability to use the post-operative theme as a marker of the success of surgery in the case of J.

In these last three extracts, the discourse on physiology has not supplied the re-definition of the patients as 'healed' which the surgeon seeks. In the light of the discussion at the end of Chapter 3 it is fairly clear that one reason for this must be that surgery does harm at the same time that it reduces illness, and that it can have serious consequences for patient fitness. From extract 4.9 (p. 83) it can be seen how direct patient intervention into the discourse on physiology can become problematic if not carefully controlled. For this reason, surgeons usually confine themselves to the other themes in their interactions with patients. In the next sections it will be seen how surgeons use strategies to control discourse in situations where patients have a greater input.

Theme 2: the discourse on wound condition

The second theme, while concerned with the physiological outcome of the surgical intervention is differentiated from the previous theme on a number of grounds:

1 It is consequential upon the surgery, not upon the condition of the patient in a wider sense.
2 It is a marker that surgery has been carried out, that the patient is no longer in the pre-operative state.
3 It is a theme upon which nursing staff and possibly the patient have an input.

Wound condition therefore plays an intermediary role between the discourse on physiology, which objectifies the patient, bracketing her/his social and individual characteristics, and the theme of recovery and discharge, which more explicitly recognizes the patient as possessing a social position, and one which soon will remove the patient from the surgical space. This theme – of the condition of the surgical wound – refers back to the operation, but in so doing acknowledges that the patient is no longer in her/his pre-operative situation, and that healing has taken place. From this perspective, it is expected that this theme would form an important discursive element in the re-categorization process.

Inspection of the wound is a regular part of the post-operative ward round. If the round is within the first 48 hours after surgery the dressing will be the one put on by the surgical team at the conclusion of the operation. The consultant may take the opportunity to remove this dressing on the round:

4.11

[*Patient C. has undergone surgery to remove an ovarian cyst. The surgeon Mrs A. is seeing her the day following.*]

MRS A.: Hello Mrs C., we have sorted out your problem for you. Let us have a look at your tummy.

[*Staff nurse and junior doctor pull curtains around, Mrs C. is laid flat, and the dressing is removed.*]

MRS A.: Yes, that's OK. You will not have much of a scar there. [1]

PATIENT C.: Thank you. When can I go home?

MRS A.: We'll see you on Monday [2] [*to nurse*] Can I have a —— [type of dressing] please?

[*Consultant and house doctor dress the wound with gauze and lengths of plaster.*]

Sometimes the task of dressing the wound is left to the nursing staff, while the ward round moves on; in this case the original dressing is only partially removed, sufficient for the consultant to see the wound. Inspecting the wound provides an opportunity, as in the previous case, to refer back to the operation to indicate its 'success' [1]. It can also enable discussion of issues of recovery and discharge to be aired. However, in the case of Mrs C. this is deemed an inappropriate development of the discourse, and, with the patient flat on her back, the issue is side-stepped [2]. In the case of Miss A., a young patient who has undergone a minor operation, the wound inspection is used to promote the discourse on discharge:

4.12

MRS A. [*looking at case notes, speaking to house doctor but across the patient*]: I think Miss A. can go home today. Can we just have a quick look, doctor . . . . How are you feeling?

PATIENT A.: OK.

[*Mrs A. looks at the condition of the surgical wound.*]

MRS A.: Well you can go home today, have you someone coming?

PATIENT A.: Yes.

MRS A.: Well that's OK. Sort that out will you, doctor?

This extract demonstrates how the discourse on the wound enables a distancing from the patient – the main discussion is between surgeon and other staff, not with the patient. It is thus unlike the discourse on discharge, where the discussion is between surgeon and patient, as will be seen in the next section.

Even when discharge is not imminent, the discourse on the wound does enable a degree of normalization of the patient following surgery:

4.13

[*Mr D. inspected a wound dressing on the lower abdomen of patient M., an old man treated for a hernia four days previously.*]

MR D.: Your wound is healing well Mr M. I want you to get about a bit. You can have a bath, but try not to get the dressing wet.

The discourse on the wound thus provides a normalization signifying the change from pre- to post-operative state. The patient can bath (i.e. normal behaviour), although in order for Mr M. to avoid wetting the dressing will require him to have a very shallow bath indeed! In some cases, the discourse is used to subvert possible difficult questions by focusing specifically on the detail of the wound.

4.14

[*Patient N. is an unhappy looking woman who has had surgery for carcinoma of the lower bowel, she is sitting on her bed, and appears to have anticipated the round as an important event: she has put make-up on.*]

MR D. [*to researcher*]: This one is a bit of a hypochondriac. She has no colon left, and her urine comes into a bag too. [*He sits down on the bed, but no move is made to examine the patient.*] How is the ileostomy?
PATIENT N.: It's much better, at least this one works.
MR D.: Good.
PATIENT N.: —— [*tries to ask a question, but Mr D. has moved away and has initiated a conversation with the house doctor.*]
MR D.: We'll see you on Tuesday.

The importance of the wound in referring back to the operation is seen in the following case in a dramatic way. Patient S. had been recovering from an abdominal operation when unexpectedly her wound burst. Despite this disaster, the discourse is constituted in such a way as to continuously refer, often in technicalities beyond the patient, to the 'successful' outcome of the surgery.

4.15
[*Patient S. is sitting in an armchair – she is looking quite distraught.*]
MR O.: Hello, Mrs D.; well we were going to send you home yesterday weren't we, thank the God almighty we didn't.
PATIENT S. [*quietly*]: No.
MR O.: Well we just don't know why this happened, there's no infection, no haematoma, nothing at all to cause this. You were up and walking . . . ?
NURSE: Yes she was walking about, and went to the lavatory and was straining, and then . . .
MR O.: . . . Yes, I hear there was small intestine hanging out. Well, you've had a nasty time, and we'll keep you in for ten days.
PATIENT S. [*aghast*]: Ten . . . days . . . ?
MR O.: Yes, but there's absolutely nothing the matter inside; we don't know why this happened, so we'll keep you in for ten days.

Inspection of the wound is a moderately frequent occurrence on post-operative rounds. The main concern is with infection, and this needs to be quickly identified. When there is satisfactory healing, no great deal is made of wound condition, and it appears that this discourse is used only when the final theme – on recovery/discharge – is inappropriate. The discourse on the wound is a way of referring to the 'success' of surgery, even when the more obvious marker of success, discharge – which of course is a strong indicator of success, is not yet a possible topic for interaction, perhaps because of the severity of the surgery, complications, or the lack of fitness of the patient as a consequence of the ordeal of surgical trauma. Wound condition is used as a means of avoiding moves into a discussion of recovery/discharge in circumstances when the surgeon would be unable to offer a positive response. Sometimes, as has been seen above, a discourse on wound condition becomes a discourse on discharge: not only has the surgery been successful, but also the injury caused has been quickly resolved and on both counts the skill of the surgeon is demonstrated.

The wound is a marker which is metonymic, which stands for the surgical operation. It is the physical sign that surgery has taken place, and its condition de-centres attention from resection which is no longer visible. When there is still underlying pathology, little concern is paid to the wound, as was seen in the section on the discourse on physiology. When pathology has been resolved, the injuries inflicted must also be allowed to heal, or the success of the resection could be compromised, as seen in the last extract. Only when the wound is satisfactorily healing can the third discourse be initiated, in which surgical healing can be defined as complete, not by reference back to the surgery itself, but forward to the next phase of the patient's biography.

Theme 3: the discourse on recovery and discharge

Discharge from hospital is a topic which most patients seek to place at the top of the agenda of the ward round. This can place them in opposition to surgeons during ward rounds, and a number of techniques which are used by surgeons to subvert this attempt have already been documented. However, the theme is one which will be instigated by surgeons at a time suited to them. The authority of the surgeon extends throughout the post-operative period, in her/his ascribed moral right to determine an appropriate date of discharge. The surgeon declares how well the patient is recovering, and may or may not suggest a discharge date. When a date is fixed the pleasure on the part of the patient which derives from this decision, in conjunction with the authoritarian nature of the discourse on recovery and discharge gives the air of a benevolent despotism to these interactions.

In the immediate period following an operation, the surgeon may choose to make statements to the patient about how s/he is recovering, without mentioning any possible discharge:

4.16
[*Patient G., an old man, had had an appendicectomy, and the removal of a tumour from his abdomen discovered during the surgery. Mr D. is cheerful.*]
MR D.: We will have you up in three weeks, and by then we will know what it is that we took out.
[*The patient appears to accept this version, although it provides no information about the tumour.*]

4.17
[*Patient H. had a stone removed from the bile duct, and although still very jaundiced is very happy that his operation is over. Mr D. is concerned to discover the reason for the stone, and is asking a range of questions about the patient's family history. He allows the conversation to be subverted.*]

PATIENT H. [*looking at the gall stone which he has in a jar by his bedside*]: Where was it?

DR D.: It was in the little tube that links the gall bladder to your intestine.

PATIENT H.: Will it come back?

DR D.: It's possible.

PATIENT H.: Was it to do with my diet?

DR D. [*laughing*]: No. Just wait till the first time you see ice cream or cream.

In both these cases the patient is supplied with information which confirms that he is recovering, and while the operation supplies the hook for the conversation, the emphasis is upon the future.

When the patient expects to be considered for discharge, this emphasis becomes central, but now a further element is added to the discourse. Up to now the surgeon's locus of activity and concern has been limited to the patient's body. Now, this area is widened, to include the patient's future biography, and his position within society – explicitly her/his home and familial arrangements.

4.18

[*Patient T. has no post-operative problems, but her circumstances are slightly unclear.*]

MRS A.: Hello, Mrs T., well I think that you can go home.

PATIENT T.: Go home today?

MRS A.: Yes I think so, where do you live?

PATIENT T.: In [district] . . .

MRS A.: . . . near, yes . . . have you someone coming?

PATIENT T.: Yes my husband is coming.

MRS A.: Yes ring him to tell him to come this afternoon, and we'll see you in a week for the stitches.

4.19

[*Patient W. is an old man who has had a major resection for gastric carcinoma. Mr D. plans to send him home if he can be looked after.*]

RESEARCHER: Are you sending him home to die?

MR D.: Oh no, I *think* I've cured him. Cancer of the stomach is not that difficult to treat, although in the long term prospects are not good. [*moving over to patient*] Who's going to look after you when you get out?

PATIENT W. [*smiling*]: You tell me when I can go, and I'll arrange to be looked after.

MR D. [*smiling*]: That's right . . . but seriously though . . . ?

PATIENT W.: Well my sister. She's older than me of course, but . . .

MR D.; Well someone to cook for you?

PATIENT W.: Oh yes, that'll be all right.

MR D.: Make a clinic appointment for next Wednesday and you can go home now.

PATIENT W.: When?

MR D.: As soon as you can arrange it.

PATIENT W. [*pretends to get out of bed*]: Well I'll give a ring now . . . [*very pleased*] Thank you.

MR D. [*joking*]: At least we're not sending you for convalescence, terrible place, worse than here. If you go for convalescence you don't need convalescence.

In the above example, Mr D. uses a search procedure in order to find excuses for discharging the patient, and the joking relationship enables them to cast off a previous relationship which had been orientated toward the operation and the patient's illness. Despite the strange definition of 'cured' used by Mr D. (recognizing the likelihood of metastasis), and with the recognition that further informal care is needed by this old man, the discourse re-constitutes W. as 'healed'.

While surgeons utilize search procedures to assemble a case for discharge, patients' attempts to supply such information when the surgeon has decided against immediate discharge founder. Patient Z. was an old lady who had had a major gynaecological procedure, and whose recovery had been slower than expected:

4.20

MRS A.: Hello, Mrs Z., I think you can go home on Monday.

PATIENT Z.: On Monday, not today?

MRS A.: No, I think we'll keep you in till Monday. [*To house doctor*] Doctor, can you listen to her tummy? Where do you live Mrs Z.?

PATIENT Z.: In [district] . . .

MRS A.: On your own?

PATIENT Z.: Yes, but I've arranged for my sisters to come over to me . . .

MRS A.: . . . Yes. [*To house doctor*] Does that sound OK?

HOUSE DOCTOR: Yes, it's OK.

PATIENT Z.: . . . they're nurses. They're not actually working any more, but they're qualified nurses . . .

MRS A.: Yes, you can go on Monday.

This extract indicates that despite the more 'patient-centred' orientation of this theme, surgeons still set the agenda on recovery/discharge, as with the other themes. There is an apparent conflict for the surgeon here. On one hand, s/he must take into account the weakened state of the post-operative patient. On the other, discharge is evidence of the new status which the post-operative patient holds, and therefore is an attractive option for the surgeon. The following extract indicates one way in which the discourse on recovery was utilized to resolve this conflict. Mr D's ward round had arrived at patient Y., who had developed a slight pyrexia (raised temperature):

4.21

MR D. [*to patient, looking at chart*]: Hello Mr Y. Well we want to send you home, but I don't like that raised temperature. [1]

PATIENT Y.: No.

MR D.: I don't know what can be causing it. We've cultured the wound and there's no infection there. I just don't know what's causing it . . . . Are things ready for you to go home?

PATIENT Y.: Yes, my wife can come and collect me today.

MR D.: Can you go to bed, and she can look after you?

PATIENT Y.:Yes.

MR D.: I don't like that raised temperature. [2] Phone your wife and you can go home now.

PATIENT Y.: Thank you very much.

Mr D. uses the phrase, 'I don't like that raised temperature' twice in this short interchange, but whereas at [1] the meaning imparted is that the raised temperature is possibly a complication which should be resolved before discharge, at [2] it has changed its meaning, and now the pyrexia is an annoying detail which is preventing the return to home and the categorization of healed, Mr D's dislike of it means he can ignore it and thus allow the patient home!

It is of course the prerogative of any patient to discharge her/himself against medical wishes. Despite this, surgeons behave as if they can control the movement of the patient. Using the discourse on discharge is a further way in which surgeons mark themselves as the people who can define post-operative patients. The decision on discharge is the final act in the process by which a patient has passed through the surgical enterprise. A surgeon has defined her/him as needing surgery, now a surgeon has made the definition of the patient as no longer needing the benefit of surgical healing, of being healed.

Discussion

The ethnography of ward round interactions analysed in terms of the three themes of physiology, wound condition and recovery/discharge, demonstrates that surgeons routinely constitute two important foci in the categorization of their patients: the operative procedure and the state of being healed. The discourse on recovery/discharge is the most forward-looking, focusing on the new status of the patient as a success of surgical healing. Where patients have not progressed to a stage where this discourse is possible, their progress is assessed in terms of physiological condition (the removal of sickness) and wound condition (one marker of the reduction in fitness caused by surgical injury). Both of these discourses choose their own ground upon which to evaluate surgical 'success';

the resection itself and the recovery of lost fitness respectively. Patients who threaten to become aberrant, such as S. whose wound had burst (extract 4.15), move back from the discharge discourse to one on wound condition, or move sideways out of the surgical gaze, as with P., the patient who was to be treated medically (extract 4.5) and the patient O. who arrested on the table (extract 4.8), who was marginalized and re-categorized as a medical or IT problem.

So there is a hierarchy to the three themes, with recovery/discharge the most clear-cut in terms of 'success', followed by wound and physiology. The latter is the most surgeon-centred, and denies patient input to the greatest extent. During the field work, the physiological detail of a case was never discussed with a patient except occasionally in terms of return to normal function post-operatively (e.g. ability to have a normal sex life or eat normal diet). Paradoxically, this is the discursive theme where the patient might have the greatest opportunity to contest the surgical conclusions, as an 'expert' on how their body normally performs. The discomfort and pain, immobility and depressed bodily functions offer quite different messages as to the nature of what the process of resection has achieved. Similarly, with the wound, the gross insult which has been inscribed on the surface of the skin during surgery, is something upon which a patient might be expected to have some comment. However, in these areas, the patient is not permitted to comment. Only when it comes to discharge may a patient have input into the discourse.

Even here, the kinds of inputs expected of a patient are limited. Surgeons make decisions on discharge by means of searches for relevant information on home arrangement, if a patient presses the right buttons (someone to collect, carer – preferably female – to look after the patient), then discharge will be eased. Any opinion a patient has on her/his discharge is not even elicited, let alone taken into account.

Post-operative ward rounds thus demonstrate surgeons at their most authoritarian. During field work only one patient was seen to manage to even briefly set an agenda for the interaction, and had to write down her questions in order to ensure they were answered. Extract 4.9 (page 83) demonstrated how a perceptive question shook the surgeon's claim to authority, which had constituted surgical 'success' as the maintenance of the patient's reproductive capabilities. This authoritarianism would suggest that for surgeons the post-operative period is an anxious time, during which their ability to define their work as success is most open to alternative definition. As revealing here, as has been noted elsewhere in this study, are the silences. There is no discussion with patients, once surgery has taken place, of the pre-operative state, or of details of the operation, or of physiological prognosis. For patients who are moving satisfactorily towards discharge, all the talk focuses on the future, and the new condition that the patient will possess as an 'ex-surgical patient'. For those who have not yet achieved this stage of progression, the discourse is guarded, focusing on very specific objectives such as the attainment of stability or the healing of the surgical wound. Patients who do not permit any of these discursive themes to be developed may be marginalized. In cases where no possible definition of success is possible, there is silence.

The ward round is thus a tightly controlled routine. The rhetoric of the processional form which rounds traditionally adopt has not been studied in this chapter in any detail thus far, and it is worth bearing in mind how the ordered procedures, and the props – file trolley, charts, curtains, and of course the patients neatly in their beds or seated next to them – contribute to this control. Most tightly controlled is what may be said, by patients in particular. Patients are disruptive elements, capable of challenging an otherwise shared discourse on surgical healing. Only once they are well on their way out of the surgical space are they permitted to have any say over what has happened to them.

At the end of Chapter 3, an exercise in deconstruction suggested that the opposition between surgery as a healing process and surgery as an injurious process lay at the root of the complexities of the relations of surgeon, anaesthetist and patient. Having survived resection, to return to the ward, this opposition around the condition of the patient still has power. By negating the negation (surgery as injury), by careful discursive procedures, the surgeon is able to sustain a definition of the post-operative patient as a success of surgery, and of course in the process, the definition of her/himself as a successful and powerful healer. The discursive strategies never leave the surgeon open to a threat of alternative definition. When the situation is its most grim, as with patient J. in IT (extract 4.10 on p. 84) who may not survive, there is silence, a grasped hand, a recourse to pure will in the face of defeat.

The deconstruction suggests that it is this will to power, through the high-risk strategy that is surgery, that guides the surgeon. Her/his denial of the injurious nature of this enterprise, her/his strategies to avoid definitions based on this pole of the opposition, are the means by which the risks to the patient do not also become risks to the authority of the surgeon to carry out healing. Surgeons take more risks than other healers, by the nature of their enterprise. Because they are skilful not only at the business of resection, but also in managing discourse, they also can claim the greater prizes in terms of authority and prestige. The techniques of surgery, as has been seen in earlier chapters, provide powerful markers for the treatment that surgeons offer, in a way which is less obvious in non-surgical medical interventions. So long as the focus is on the good that surgery does, not upon the injury, then surgeons can reap the benefits of their powerful healing technique. The discourses used on ward rounds illustrate one way that focus on good is sustained.

5

THE MANAGEMENT OF SURGERY

ANAESTHETIST DR J.: Consultative mechanisms in the management process foster bad, non-professional thinking.

Introduction

The surgeon, in common with almost all doctors in Western medical culture, claims a right to autonomy of action – a right enshrined in the Hippocratic Oath with its requirement that the well-being of her/his patient be the primary and over-riding concern of a doctor's practice. This claim has been the subject of a vast area of discourse within medical sociology – with Parsons' (1951) five attributes of the doctor role as avatar. On the other hand, surgeons, like all doctors working in the UK within the NHS hospital service, must perforce accept the constraints upon action imposed by an institution and its management, and the resources which it controls and allocates. In this chapter this apparent contradiction between clinical autonomy and managerial constraint is examined, based on ethnography and interviews with staff at General Hospital during the field work. Specifically, the focus within the analysis is upon the 'inefficiencies' in delivery of surgery on a daily basis which was mentioned in passing in Chapter 2. This feature of surgery – the daily interruptions, delays and over-running of lists – is immediately obvious to anyone who gains extended access to an operating theatre over an extended period. These apparent inefficiencies in the service are surprising, as one might expect the routinization which is so evident in hospitals in terms of patient timetables (Roth, 1963; Zerubavel, 1979) to extend throughout the institution. Consequently, it is appropriate to devote some space to this datum, and to use it to focus on the issues concerned in the management of surgery.

An objective of any system of management is the resolution of day-to-day anomalies or problems which arise within an organization. Most organizations in the West possess characteristics of the modern era: rationalization, progress and efficiency, according to Parker. However (Parker, 1990, p. 8),

> ... the rationalities deployed within an organization are relative and collective. There is [*sic*] no absolute criteria for truth and wisdom inside or outside any given organization, and those 'truths' that are utilised are continually subject to renegotiation and re-encoding by others within the organization

In this perspective the smooth running of a service such as surgery will depend upon the maintenance of shared local rationalities by management, clinicians and others involved. Disruption and the breakdown of order would reflect a failure to sustain these shared rationalities. So by looking at the points at which failure of order occurs should enable an understanding of the extent of shared interpretations of the surgical enterprise, and the positions held by different groups which do not coincide. In the course of this chapter, the ethnographic data will be subjected to two exercises in deconstruction: firstly of the discourses of personnel with both clinical and management responsibilities, and secondly of the differing positions of clinicians and managers with regard to the day-to-day and the more strategic level of organization of surgery. I will return to this discussion of organizations at the end of this chapter.

General Hospital forms the principal component of the acute Unit of its District, and since the Griffiths re-organization of the NHS, administration at General Hospital has been the responsibility of a Unit General Manager. The three areas relevant to the management of surgery on a day-to-day basis are managed by:

1 *General Services Manager*: responsible (*inter alia*) for distribution of supplies.
2 *Patient Services Manager*: responsible for out-patients, admissions, bed information and records.
3 *Clinical Services Manager*: responsible for staffing and running of clinical areas, who in turn delegates to the *Operating Department Manager* (ODM), responsible for surgical operating suites, and to the *Night Services Manager*.

Managing the five twin surgical operating suites is a considerable operation, entailing control of 120 nursing and auxiliary staff (88.34 full-time equivalents) during day shifts, the provision of supplies ranging from sterile dressings to equipment hardware and the regulation of the supply of patients to the theatres 24 hours a day. The coordination of these three elements derives ultimately upon the ODM. Within each theatre suite responsibility for staff rotas and control of patient lists is delegated to the theatre sister. The sister deputizes for the ODM when the latter is off duty. With this brief resume of management structure, the focus will now turn to the episodes when this structure is stressed and breaks down.

TABLE 5.1 Initiators of disruptive episodes

Delay in patient arrival in theatre
Management
Porter unavailable
Ward nurse escort unavailable
Patient processing not complete, e.g. case notes, consent, late arrival in hospital
Surgeon
Patient is not called until previous operation completed
Patient processing not complete, e.g. case notes, consent, late arrival in hospital
Anaesthetist/Surgeon
Patient has not been pre-medicated

Delay in induction
Patient history suggests contraindications for anaesthesia not anticipated prior to arrival
   in OT, due to:
Surgeon
Late addition to list
Change in procedure
Anaesthetist/Surgeon
Anaesthetist has not seen patient in advance
Patient not pre-medicated
Uncertainty
Clinical signs elicited on arrival
Induction complexity greater than anticipated

Delay in commencing operation
Surgeons
Surgical staff not scrubbed
Instrumentation not ready due to change in procedure
Management
Nursing shortage

Increase in operation time
Uncertainty
Exploratory procedure reveals need for further procedure
Complication or unforeseen complexity arises
Crisis management

Operating session runs over limits
Surgeon
Additional elective patients on list
Induction time not accounted for in planning list
Overall operating time underestimated

The disruption of surgical routine

The routine of the surgical day at General Hospital, which as has been seen in
Chapter 2 is concerned with the processing of patients through the surgical

enterprise, is regularly disrupted by a remarkable component of apparent inefficiency and unpredictability. Patients arrive late, or not at all, patients are precipitately removed from lists or substituted by ones with quite different procedures, procedures are not those planned and written into the list, no account of anaesthetic time is made, too many patients are scheduled and lists are unmanageable or last into the evening, instruments are unavailable and not ready at the same time as the patient. In the earliest stages of this ethnography of surgery at General, a first morning of observation in which a surgical list of four patients inexplicably diminished to two cases, separated by a long delay, left the researcher with an assumption that these unpredictable alterations and delays were anomalous, an accidental consequence of the uncertainty of the surgical process. This impression was bolstered by the virtual absence of any discussion between OT staff on the subject. During delays or interruptions, staff would retire to offices or the rest room and make desultory conversation. Unless coaxed, the delays seemed to be something which OT staff either considered so commonplace as not worth mentioning, or about which for some reason they preferred not to speak.

The discovery that this pattern of delays was in fact the norm came only after a period of familiarization and questioning of informants among OT staff during the course of field work. In Chapter 2 a number of such episodes were documented, and I refer the reader to extract 2.22, concerning Dr. J. (p. 35) which concerns a regular delay due to a lack of a nurse to accompany a patient, extract 2.23, concerning a last-minute change to a surgical procedure (IUA) on p. 36 and the long extract 2.27 on p. 37 which provides a concatenation of events: a change of surgical procedure, an addition of a patient to a list, a disappearing patient and a problem over anaesthesia. These extracts give a flavour, and other examples are described in the following pages. Based on the total experience of surgery during the field work, the range of reasons for delays have been classified into a typology in Table 5.1.

Once encouraged, one informant – the anaesthetist Dr J. – became an enthusiastic commentator upon the inefficiencies witnessed in theatre, and his discursive use of them to define the moral and intellectual superiority of anaesthetists over surgeons has already been noted in Chapter 3. Dr J. was willing to implicate a wide range of actors as blameworthy, from nurses

5.1

ANAESTHETIST DR J.: That call was from the ward – there's no-one to come up to theatre with the patient. That usually means that the staff nurse has not planned ahead.

a combination of patients and nurses

5.2

DR J.: Patients are called by letter, and will or will not agree to come in. Sometimes it's difficult to arrange substitutes, but it means you cannot plan with any confidence that the list will be as proposed. Some surgeons anticipate this, and send for more patients than they would expect to get. Then they have too many, and this is irritating if it happens too often. It's a problem for nursing staff, who are very rigid.

or anyone and everyone

5.3

DR J.: It's a problem having to think for everybody. You suppose that everyone knows what they are doing, but much of the time they don't seem to.

However, Dr J. saved his particular blame for the incompetences of surgeons.

5.4

DR J.: There was absolute chaos here [plastic theatre] yesterday. The list was arranged so that patients were due in theatre hours before they came to hospital. Then in the afternoon, two major cases were put on the list – which meant there was not enough time without keeping staff on after six, and it had to be re-arranged, so one case is being done today instead.

5.5

DR, J.: Two or three per cent of patients will have a problem [which makes anaesthesia risky] which cannot be sorted out. The anaesthetist needs to see the patient, but some firms [of surgeons] seem incapable of concocting a list until the morning of the schedule.

This attribution was not simply vitriol on the part of Dr J., other anaesthetists were also willing to blame surgeons, and the cooperation seen in Chapter 3 certainly did not mean that clinicians stuck together.

5.6

ANAESTHETIST DR C.: The surgeon does not consider the anaesthesia to be anything other than wasted time. They don't take it into account. . . . Surgeons regard the theatre as their own, they say what will go on.

In contrast, and not surprisingly, surgeons select other targets to explain delays. They reject any suggestion they are to blame, and implicate staff outside the OT, patients or their over-worked juniors.

5.7

SURGEON MR Y.: This [a particularly long delay of over an hour] is the sort of thing that happens. The consultant tells the staff nurse [to

arrange a patient to sign a consent form, in this case], who tells the
houseman, who forgets, or is too busy.

5.8
SURGEON MRS A.: I can't believe it, the man came [to collect a tissue biopsy]
and the secretary sent him away. He came all the way from [———]
himself and she sent him away.

5.9
SURGEON MR M.: Here we are [in the rest room], all ready to do our work,
and we wait on the ministrations of the porter to bring us our work.

Where there is no obvious culprit the disruption is ascribed to general social
forces or as a fault of bureaucracy:

5.10
MRS A.: That's the trouble with this country, no-one will do anything
properly.

5.11
SURGEON MR T.: Yes, there is quite a lot of hanging around, that's the price
of being part of a large organization.

Surgeons are defensive about their own culpability, and will seek to shift the
blame, with the uncertainty of surgery supplying not only the excuse but also by
implication a vindication of their clinical judgement.

5.12
MR Y.: Orthopaedic surgery at General Hospital is on take seven days a
week, so there are always emergencies. A list is made up at very short
notice. There are patients in the wards, and we decide to add them to a
list. People say that they don't have to go on *this* list, but they have to go
on *a* list. That's what people forget.

Nurses working in general usually took the anaesthetist's perspective with the
surgeon as culprit in the disruption of routines.

5.13
NURSE J.: Orthopaedic surgeons are the worst, they arrange things at the
last minute, and then they're not organized properly. They don't
communicate. It's probably because most of them are foreign – they
don't understand each other.

5.14
INTENSIVE THERAPY UNIT NURSE C.: Thoracic surgeons do not readily
give up their rights and responsibility for a patient who comes into

Intensive Therapy after an operation, because they see it as the slippery slope towards death.

5.15

NURSE J.: Mr [–] will never call for the next patient to be brought from the ward until the current patient is virtually sewn up. That can mean a long delay, as the ward may not be geared to immediately jump to it.

5.16

ANAESTHETIST DR W.: I don't usually know who is on the list until I arrive, so I don't usually give pre-meds.

NURSE J.: They never give orthopaedic patients pre-meds.

DR W.: Surgeons never know till the last minute who is on the list.

These commentaries from different members of staff in the OT suggest that there are a variety of explanations for why disruption occurs. The typology of delay developed in Table 5.1, based on observations and interviews, indicates that indeed the activities of surgery enables a wide range of disruptors. The intention here is not really to try to discover the 'truth' about this disruption, the variety of possible disruptions identified in the figure makes the point that all members of OT staff have the potential to disrupt, with surgeons apparently having the most 'opportunities', and certainly the field work observations gave some support to the view that surgeons had a significant degree of responsibility for interrupting the proceeding of surgical lists.

While uncertainty deriving from the unpredictability of the conduct of surgical cases is a regular feature of the daily activities of the OT, any disruption occurring as a consequence was observed to be accepted by those involved in the business of surgery as legitimate, if unfortunate.

5.17

A patient was having varicose veins stripped out of her legs by a consultant and a senior registrar. This procedure entails the insertion of an instrument into the vein which can then be pulled to strip the vein out. The veins kept tearing during this procedure, so that little could be extracted at a time, and the instrument had to be continually rethreaded into the veins. This considerably added to the time taken. All staff accepted this as something which could not be blamed on anything other than the uncertainty of a particular patient's anatomy.

Operation theatre staff share a perspective on the cause of delay in events where an outsider can be blamed, and a label of inefficiency or incompetence can be attributed.

5.18

Staff in the OT rest room were drinking coffee while they waited for the next patient on the list to arrive. The problem was attributed to the portering staff, who according to the discussion were never available, or who claimed that they had other duties to attend to.

This review of discourses on delays suggests a wide variety of ascriptions of blame. While surgeons are regularly blamed for delays, they themselves reject that their actions are anything other than legitimate. They perceive last-minute arrangements or changes to lists, changes in procedure, over-loading lists and ignoring preparation time as hazards of their uncertain job. For them, those who are to blame are ward nurses and porters, who are not available to ferry patients into the OT, anaesthetists for taking too long in induction and preparation, or patients who do not appear for their surgery. A simple demarcation might therefore be made between surgeons and other staff in the OT as to the attribution of blame for delays and disruption, and on that basis it would theoretically be possible, given the right information, to decide whether surgeons were falsely pointing the finger away from themselves as the prime instigators of the disruption. This of course would require of the enthographer some skill at determining the 'real' cause of disruption, and apart from the fact that I almost certainly do not have that skill, it must be clear from this book that the interest is less with what 'really' happens, and more with how people involved in surgery construct events within their particular discourses, and the points at which those discourses seem frayed at the edges, incapable of sustaining the claims to authority which they are intended to constitute.

In this perspective, the way forward for analysis is to examine discontinuities within the various discourses, and ask questions which probe these gaps. Why for instance, *do surgeons not ascribe blame to the higher echelons of management* for inefficiencies? Management are not present (they are a favourite whipping-boy for the disaffected), and according to the extract from Parker quoted on p. 95, have a discourse on what they are trying to organize which is extremely limited in its applicability. Is there something about the management of the surgical service which surgeons find difficult to criticize, that to do so would be to criticize surgery itself? To consider this possibility, this chapter now looks at the management discourse on surgery and on surgical disruption.

Management and disruption of routine

From a management perspective, it is to be expected that control and maintenance of the routines of surgery would be identified as principal objectives, and that a failure of routines in day-to-day running of theatres would be a cause for concern. Three operating department managers (ODM) were interviewed on the topic of the daily management of the OT. The General Hospital ODM is nurse F., while the other two were both consultant anaesthetists and part-time ODMs: one for the General's day surgery unit, Dr

F., the other, the obstetrics ODM for a nearby hospital, Dr M. Nurse F. concentrated on issues of resources:

5.19

NURSE F.: The work of the ODM entails a big personnel management task. The day in theatre is 8 a.m. to 5 p.m.; two or three nurses will work a half-day, the others come on the late shift. I make sure that the work gets organized to make the best use of staff. From time to time I look at scheduling, to make efficient use of theatres, and I monitor the amount of emergency operating in sessions.

Dr M. offers a different emphasis, patient-centred as opposed to resource-centred:

5.20

DR M.: Emergencies are more of an administrative than a medical emergency. If we are running an efficient unit, we want to run nurses, anaesthetists and equipment all the time. So we fill all the theatres nine to five with elective surgery. If an emergency arises, we need to break into the elective list, and then find extra time for the elective surgery. Surgeons prefer to let the emergencies build up, and then do a list overnight. But that is awful for the patients, because the surgery will be done by on-call surgeons. The alternative is to have three theatres open in the evening – but most of the time two will lie unused.

Dr M. and nurse F. also had different perceptions of the reasons surgical operating routines are disrupted. Dr M. apparently continued to perceive himself as a clinician with an interest in the strategic level of management. It was threats to disruption of these longer-term plans rather than the day-to-day routine which he identified, pointing to general uncertainty, to out-dated traditions, and to higher management as the principal obstacles to efficiency.

5.21

DR M.: One of the things that is worrying clinicians about management, with all the new management exercises, is that one is playing the numbers game – there is no measure of quality. For instance, regional management noted there was no orthopaedic day case surgery at [Hospital W]. The reason is that it's in the middle of nowhere – but management do not understand that. One of my reasons for getting involved in management was to bring in some clinical judgements.

5.22

DR M.: There is an attempt to reduce waiting lists currently. The trouble is if you reduce them to nothing, then the surgical service is dependent on the ebb and flow of what comes through the door. So you instigate an appointment system booking three months ahead. All the lists are full, but if a couple of emergencies appear, you have to cancel some, and the cancellations go to the bottom of the list again. In orthopaedics, beds are blocked by emergencies, and waiting lists then go very slowly for elective cases.

In this extract, Dr M. identifies the *smooth passage of an optimal number of patients through the OT* as the principal objective of his participation in management. Nor does he perceive disruption of surgical routine as a primary concern. Similarly, Dr F., another anaesthetist with managerial duties argued that:

5.23

DR F.: Developing day surgery is a matter of resourcing and logistics. It does entail a change in surgical practice, but not so much in terms of technique as patient management. The research that is needed concerns feasibility. . . . Doctors don't like to be told what to do by administrators. I understand the doctors and can talk to them, and also have some respect for managers. It's down to personality.

These *strategic* concerns contrast with the much more down-to-earth discourse of nurse manager F. While recognizing the strategic planning aspect, in particular resource issues such as upgrading of theatres and creation of a central instrument preparation unit to enhance patient flow through surgery, she saw the attempts to push as many patients as possible through the OT as *potentially disruptive* of routine and a serious problem requiring management input.

5.24

NURSE F.: Surgeons are prima donnas; they want theatres to be open longer however long they are open. If I had an extra ten staff things would be very different, but we are very efficient, we do not waste resources. . . . I can try to control the amount of work. I keep telling surgeons to control their lists. Recently there was a night with 12 emergency cases. Consultants in thoracic, gyne, neuro and general surgery came in, and they all wanted to operate as quickly as possible. They are only interested in their own patient and what they want to do – they are not interested in their colleagues. They wanted the staff and extra theatres to be available, and it was up to the night sister to decide who went into theatre, in which order. Fortunately she was very experienced, and got it about right, and none of the patients suffered medically. When the surgeons cool off they will realize they were selfish, but since it happened I have had the surgeons on the phone asking me to sort it out so it doesn't happen again. It can be very unpleasant in theatre. I would say that surgery is unique, and being in theatre is unique. The surgeons are not like that on the wards. Surgeons will try to take advantage day after day, and will use emotional blackmail to try to keep staff on late. One of the surgeons in plastic [theatre] says that if you want to be a theatre nurse you must not have a life of your own. That is old-fashioned!

Nurse F. thus recognizes the reality of constant interruptions to routine. In comparison, from the comments of Dr M. one might imagine that the daily disruption of surgery was something he had never experienced. Returning to the claims and counter-claims as to the origins of disruption, the discourses from these operating department managers reveal a discrepancy. Nurse manager F. sees the task as maintaining the smooth day-to-day running of a complex organization, while the two clinicians with managerial duties perceive their input to be at a strategic rather than an everyday level. The following extracts emphasize this discrepancy.

5.25

DR M.: Doctors are totally outside the management structure. Griffiths [management re-organization] thought the only way to bring them in was to involve them as managers. The consultant is still the boss, they may not be able to initiate anything but they can wreck things. For instance, moving lists is an administrative nightmare. Consultants' lists are tied up with outpatient clinics. They don't want to do a Monday morning list when no tests can be done in advance, or Friday afternoon when they do their private casework. A consultant may have taken 10 years to get the right arrangements, and will not want to change. I've been here 15 years, so if it comes to leaning on a surgeon I have the power, and I understand their concerns. If a nurse manager told a surgeon something he would say no way. It works out quite well in practice.

5.26

NURSE F.: Clinicians do not have the time to be managers, they have to give up some of their clinical commitments. They claim they want to control the staff, but without having to do any managerial work. Currently clinicians are being involved in plastic and neurosurgery management. It's a waste of my time and theirs, but its a novelty for them at the moment. They come up with ludicrous ideas, for instance that all nursing staff should work early shifts Monday to Friday, and be on call at weekends. But the staff have to have time off. And they don't understand that there have to be staff in theatre at other times to do the routine preparatory work. I can't think of one good idea that has come out of it.

For Dr M. the 'clinical' characteristics of professionalism, flexibility, personality and thoughtfulness are the useful managerial attributes he brings to the job.

Despite their managerial duties, both Dr M. and Dr F. take a position which recognizes clinical autonomy to a far greater extent than other actors. It seems therefore that, despite the inter-specialty rivalry which was recognized at the beginning of this chapter, and earlier in the book, these anaesthetists share something with their surgeon colleagues in terms of perspective. A demarcation between clinicians and 'the rest' might thus be drawn on the basis of the ethnographic extracts. Using the deconstructive methodology, what can be made of the local rationalities of these two groups? Firstly, for the clinicians:

Position: Uniqueness of patient requiring clinical assessment.
Negation: Patient is not unique, but one of many.
Negation of negation: No patient other than the one in the OT is important.
Deconstruction: Clinicians use professional responsibility as a means of organizing their work to their advantage, and to legitimate disruption.

For the 'rest':

Position: Surgical routines enable smooth running of OT.
Negation: Surgery involves uncertainty because cases are different.
Negation of negation: Planning ahead can ensure surgical routines are not disrupted.
Deconstruction: Surgical routines contribute to job satisfaction, and create a discourse of teamwork which benefits lower levels of a hierarchy.

This exercise in the analysis of the ethnography suggests that an opposition of clinical autonomy and cooperative activity has utility in understanding discourses on surgical management. Clinicians deny the need for teamwork, while 'the rest' question the ability of clinicians to make crucial decisions concerning the effective use of surgical services. Both sides use the disruption to exploit their own power struggles. However, given that clinicians in practice apparently *are* in a position to make these decisions, why have they not finally won this battle? Is their position actually more precarious that it looks? All that has been done thus far is to describe an unequal power struggle, and one which is fairly obvious. Why does the struggle have to be re-fought on a daily basis? It is therefore unfortunately not sufficient to leave the deconstruction at this stage, a further iteration of data is needed in order to understand precisely why this power struggle continues, and to locate its precise position within the relations of the surgical enterprise. To consider this further the ethnography will now focus upon the relations between the consultant clinical staff and the management structure of General Hospital.

The position of clinical staff

So far I have not looked at a discourse which may be expected to have some bearing – the 'official' version of the management of surgery. When I started to try to understand the administrative arrangements at General, I used my informant the anaesthetist Dr J. He and I studied the official diagrams of the management structure which had been circulated to 'enable staff to understand the organisation', as the covering letter had it.

5.27
RESEARCHER: There does not seem to be any mention of clinical staff in this plan.
DR J.: No . . . that's true [*looking at the diagrams, and checking to see if the researcher was correct*]. No, they are not mentioned.
RESEARCHER: Does that mean that they are not under the management of the hospital?
DR J.: Well . . . no, they aren't. They are employed by the NHS to work in the hospital.

These questions seemed to provide Dr J. with some insight which he had not previously fully recognised. To begin with he appeared taken aback, and cautious of misinforming, enquired of a colleague to check what was apparent: that the situation was indeed that there was no obvious place within the management structure for the clinical staff. My attempt to clarify this, suggesting that the doctors 'sort of float around outside this hierarchy' was accepted as appropriate and also as an apparently attractive concept. The conversation continued:

5.28
RESEARCHER: Doesn't that make it difficult for the clinicians to have an influence over the running of the hospital? You have no direct input to the Unit general manager.
DR J.: Yes I suppose that's so . . .
RESEARCHER: There is the Hospital Consultants Advisory Committee to the District general manager . . . ?
DR J.: We would give advice on an informal basis to the operating department manager . . . but that will be accepted or rejected . . . . The clinical area managers will come into contact with the consultants.

Dr J. considered this day-to-day contact with the nurse managers, and with theatre sisters, more significant than the rarefied atmosphere of the district and unit level advisory committees. The function of these advisory committees (explained from a management perspective) was outlined in an un-dated consultative document on management of General Hospital's district, subsequently supplied to me by Dr J.

5.29
THE PROVISION OF PROFESSIONAL ADVICE . . . The introduction of the general management function into the Health Service in no way diminishes the need for professional advice, particularly medical and nursing advice . . . where doctors are responsible for the decisions which commit most of the Service's resources, it would be inconceivable that it

could be managed effectively without substantial input . . . . Paradoxically, as the service becomes increasingly complex it requires . . . both general management and better advice from professionals. . . .

. . . At the Authority level, the two medical members – consultant and general practitioner – will continue to give general professional advice in a personal rather than representative capacity.

. . . At District level the consultant and general practitioner representatives will advise the District General Manager and the Management Advisory Group . . .

. . . At Unit Level, there will be at least one Medical Adviser nominated by the Unit Medical Advisory Committee or its equivalent who will advise the Unit General Manager and the Unit Management Advisory Group.

The description of these formal structures suggests that the problem of reconciling institutional constraint with clinical autonomy is resolved in the longer term, in policy and organization matters, via this concept of 'advice'. The management seeks and is provided with advice from the clinical consultants (and nursing adviser) and acts accordingly, within some management programme. The autonomy of consultants to act according to their clinical judgements is constrained by institutional factors (resources, time etc.), but these constraints are to be seen as rationalizations made by management as a consequence of the 'advice' provided by clinicians. Ethnographic data from these committees, which would obviously provide further material on the negotiations conducted between management and clinicians, are not available for analysis. However, even without going into this material, it is now possible to advance the deconstruction, by considering the local rationality which is constituted in this discourse on management at the level of strategic planning.

Position: Clinicians advise management on appropriate strategy according to judgements as to 'best patient care'.

Negation: Clinicians have no direct control over the strategy and the managerial hierarchy, and 'best patient care' is defined by management criteria.

Negation of negation: This lack of control is de-emphasized, and 'advice' from consultants is seen as a highly valued commodity in identifying policy for patient care.

Deconstruction: At the strategic level, clinicians have to compromise their clinical judgements as to patient care in order to sustain their position in the hospital hierarchy.

The deconstruction suggests that the arrangements whereby consultants advise management put them in a difficult position. No doubt most of the time their clinical judgements will be addressed in policy, but they have no direct access to power, they depend on the reflected power of the management structure, and as such are compromised in acting entirely according to professional judgement.

Management decisions may be taken for organizational and economic reasons in addition to the clinical advice offered.

Of course, these management decisions are reflected on a day-to-day basis in organizational practice. However, now there is no need for compromise. In the operating theatre (a wonderfully isolated world in which to exert authority) the clinician can once more revert to decision-making purely on clinical judgement. Furthermore, management decisions which may act to reduce clinical power (for instance, setting work patterns or organizing waiting lists so as to limit the opportunity to do surgery according to professional judgement), can be overturned with little likelihood of direct retribution, as the representatives of management are either low in the chain of command, or clinicians in disguise!

Here is the source of disruption to surgical routine, not in the OT at all, but in the arrangements whereby consultants advise management. Conflicts which at policy level are obscured, re-appear reflected in the work and organizational practices of OT staff. Resolution which should but cannot occur at policy level is attempted in the OT, and the result is the collapse of routines. Surgeons:

1 attempt to optimalize the use of the surgical facilities, and fail to accept institutional constraints on time;
2 list patients assessed as in need of treatment at very short notice, or change procedures at short notice, with consequent problems prior to a patient's arrival in the theatre;
3 may not unreservedly release their patients into the responsibility of recovery personnel, thereby delaying the following operation.

Institutional constraints, in the form of routines of staffing and OT procedure, not only may resist these demands by surgeons, but also impose further restrictions through the consequences of managerial arrangements, such as a shortage of nursing or ancillary staff, instruments or other facilities. The differences between the two levels of interaction are summarized in Figure 5.1.

The material in earlier chapters of this book has pointed towards an analysis which suggests that surgical discourse is concerned with ensuring the passage of patients through the OT in such a way that surgeons can define the patient and her/his operation as a 'success'. In Chapter 3 the complex interactions of surgeons and anaesthetists was examined and found to mediate such claims, while the material in Chapter 4 considered how surgeons talk to and about patients post-operatively. In both cases, discourse is structured to enable the clinical judgement which has been necessary to achieve this success to be the point from which outcome is evaluated. Management policy, on the other hand, places its emphasis on efficiency as a criterion of success, ignoring these aspects of surgical discourse by which surgeons make their valuations of outcome. Any apparent shared interest between management and clinicians at policy level in achieving maximum patient throughput within available resources, is in fact illusory, based on differing conceptions and different meanings of the passage of the patient through the OT. Whereas, for management this is purely an

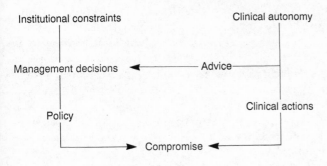

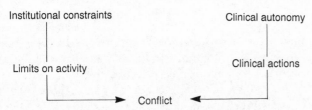

FIGURE 5.1 Institutional constraint and clinical autonomy.

instrumental interest, in which the operation is merely one part, albeit
the essential part, of the entire hospitalization process of the surgical patient. For
the surgeon this is not enough; it reduces the surgeon to a cog in a machine which
processes patients, and it defines her/his part in the process as that of a technician.
It fails to address the importance of clinical autonomy, not only upon the healing
of the patient, but also for the surgeon her/himself. It is through this clinical
autonomy that the surgeon's authority and privilege is constituted and retained.

Discussion

The preceding investigation of the management of surgery, and in particular the
disruption of operating theatre routine provides further support for the position
which is being developed throughout this book: that the activities reported in the
ethnography can be understood in terms of the daily power relations and
struggles between the actors involved in surgery, and that it is through these daily
activities that the power of surgery as a healing technique is manifested and
sustained. In this chapter, analysis has disclosed how daily interruptions to
routine reflect power struggles, not in the OT itself, but at the highest level in
hospital management. I have suggested elsewhere (Fox, 1991) that this finding
demonstrates the potential for evaluation studies using the deconstructive

methodology and the postmodern position in ethnographic analysis. Without importing complex structural theories of organization or social structure, the analysis has identified in the inefficiencies ocurring in the setting and the discourses of the various groupings involved, reflections of relations and conflicts outside the ethnographic setting, in this case between consultants and senior management. The potential of deconstruction in evaluating surgery will be addressed in Chapter 7.

Deconstruction never ends, and one topic which has not been examined in this investigation of the management of surgery concerns the position of nursing staff in relation to management within the NHS. Nurses are constrained by management in a way which clinical staff are not, but they also see themselves as having a managerial function within a hospital, if only with regard to patients and the routines which order their lives within the hospital. Nurses have been quick to see opportunities in management as a consequence of NHS re-organizations as possibilities for career enhancement or advancement, and the moves in nurse training toward an elite graduate grade recognize that management is an appropriate area for nurses to move into (Dingwall *et al.*, 1988). As has been seen, nurse managers see themselves as the legitimate and rightful heirs to senior posts in the management structure. Nurse manager F. was extremely derogatory about one senior manager who was 'only a former technician' (this being the reason for his incompetence in providing adequate supplies to the operating department of General). So there is another power struggle here, and the deconstructive strategy could no doubt select data quoted in this chapter and elsewhere in this volume to support an analysis. It may well be that gender is a factor as yet not identified in the analysis, which requires further effort.

One thing which I think comes over strongly in this section is how the methodology of deconstruction opens up new ways of looking at the data. The daily disruption of surgery was a puzzling datum which could have been easily overlooked, particularly if a researcher had a commitment to explaining social order and the functionality of organizations. As it was, it was only through careful observation and interviews with informants, deriving from a vague idea that management was something which needed to be investigated, that the disruption was ever available for analysis as other than an anomaly deriving from uncertainty, economic cutbacks or the personalities of those involved (incidentally all factors which may indeed play a part). Different perspectives might indeed come to different conclusions, holding as they do sets of assumptions. It is worth mentioning one assumption which has not been made in the analysis in this chapter (an assumption which is often made as a starting point for analysis of organizations) – that they work. Starting from this assumption, organizational analysis is thus concerned with discovering how human agency intervenes to cause inefficiency in the system, and how to resolve these aberrant elements to increase efficiency or rationality in the system. This is a very large assumption, and one which of course is applied in many settings including family therapy and process evaluation. But what happens if, following the post-modern perspective as reviewed by Parker, one starts from the opposite position, that *organization is a fragile, unstable process*, supported by discourses which provide it with a mythical sense of continuity: 'if you look for a system you will find one' (Parker, 1990, p. 6). Ultimately organizations *cannot* work because they are constituted around localized rationalities which have sense only within the institution. Organization (as a verb, not a noun) is an automatic response to an external threat, a *remedial* move in situations marked by uncertainty, disorder and imbalance (Cooper and Burrell, 1988, p. 103). The effort of influencing human agents inside or outside an institution forces these apparent 'rationalities' (which are little more than myths) into contact with differing patternings of meaning. The 'stronger' the will to organize, the less has an institution the ability to control what it wishes to control. When it seeks to influence those who threaten it, it instead threatens its own closure, the myths by which it appears to be a totality.

From this perspective disruption in an organization is to be expected, once it trys to act outside its own boundaries, and order is the surprising datum. And from such a position it becomes clear why in the absence of order, and in the silences over the limitations of the rationalities of an organization, one finds the key to the discourse which seeks to enable organization, in a way which is impossible if one focuses on the anomaly of order. This section of ethnography supplies a further element of the social meaning of surgery concerning the need for surgeons to control how they move their patients through surgery. As in Chapter 4, the positions developed here indicate the need for surgeons to control this process in order to sustain and achieve their authority. This chapter has thus shown the importance of 'clinical autonomy' for surgical discourse. Disorder in surgery occurs when this need for control can no longer be reconciled with an alternative management-inspired discourse on doing surgery. This conclusion is an extremely important one for those who would attempt to organize or manage surgery, as will be seen in Chapter 6, when I turn to a model of surgery which has not really featured so far in this study: the day case.

6

DAY CASE SURGERY

Introduction

In the early spring of 198- (year deleted to sustain anonymity), a day case surgery unit was opened at General Hospital, marking the culmination of an 18-month period of discussion and preparation which was, coincidentally, the period during which field work was being conducted. The day case option for surgical treatment was a topic which had been raised with informants throughout this period, and it was therefore particularly fortuitous from the point of view of this research that the planning and consultation process, and eventually the opening of the designated unit occurred during the fieldwork period. The visits to the day case unit were the last data to be gathered, and are also the last data to be reported in this study. The positioning of this chapter after a chapter on management will be seen to have its own logic, as the day case strategy clearly entails organizational arrangements which in many ways are unlike those for traditional in-patient surgery. But the analysis will show how many of the themes identified in this study have relevance for understanding day surgery. As such it is an appropriate place for the completion of this study of the social meaning of surgery.

Day case surgery (henceforth DCS) requires definition for the purposes of this case study. Surgery has been conducted on an out-patient or day admission basis for very many years (Royal College of Surgeons of England, 1985, p. 1), principally for very minor conditions probably not requiring general anaesthesia. More recently, patients have been selected for day surgery despite a requirement for a general anaesthetic. These cases fulfil a Royal College of Surgeons definition of a surgical day case as 'a patient who is admitted for investigation or operation on a planned non-resident basis and occupies for a period a bed in a ward or unit set aside for this purpose. The concept of "admission" is . . . retained to emphasise the need to observe proper admission procedures or records' (RCSE, 1985, p. 3).

When field work began at General a number of day cases were taking place, and were observed by the researcher, principally in plastic theatre. Some terminations of pregnancy and a range of gynaecological investigative procedures were also being conducted on a day basis in Theatre S, while some endoscopies were day cases conducted in the endoscopy theatre. Patients having these procedures would either be admitted to a ward, or would be taken to the anaesthetic room directly. Both theatres had recovery rooms which doubled as a 'ward' from which these patients would be discharged. However, for the purposes of this study, the definition of DCS excludes these cases, DCS here is used to mean only *those cases admitted to a designated DCS unit on a planned non-resident basis*. This definition has been adopted in order to control the case study for theoretical reasons which will now be outlined.

By its very nature, day surgery emphasizes the operation, and by limiting the hospital stay to a few hours before and after the procedure, de-emphasizes these periods. As was seen in Chapter 4, the post-operative period is an important one for defining patients as healed, but contrariwise, other earlier material showed how surgeons regard the operation itself as paramount, often at the expense of relations with staff who prepare patients and deal with them in the immediate post-operative period. Thus DCS provides an interesting paradox: on the basis of these findings DCS will be either highly prized as a strategy for demonstrating healing, or denigrated as a process which denies the discursive activities which mark surgery as more than just a technical intervention carried out by a rude mechanical. It will also be recalled in relation to the material in Chapter 5 that the demands which surgeons make on surgical management to control the throughput of patients lead to conflict where these demands oppose the management/nursing definition of the surgical enterprise. In DCS, whose definition of how to do surgery has triumphed? DCS is part of a discourse on efficiency, pushing as many patients through the hospital as can physically be included on a list, avoiding at least one limitation: that imposed by availability of beds – the unit being designed to ensure enough trolley space for all pre-surgical and recovering patients treated during a day-long list. A patient on a DCS list may have been discharged before the list upon which s/he was included has even been completed. The surgeon may see her/him only when unconscious upon the table, particularly if the pre-operative examination is conducted by a junior. Have surgeons and management resolved the differences identified in Chapter 5? If so, then DCS will not be affected by the disruption and conflict reported in traditional surgery at General. And will this definition be shared by nursing staff, for whom the patient's healing is defined through the process of care (pre- and post-operatively) during the stay in hospital?

These issues will be examined by recourse to the ethnography of the routines of the DCS unit, through consideration of the context which led to the opening of the unit, and through interview material elicited prior to the unit opening, and comments of staff working in the unit subsequently.

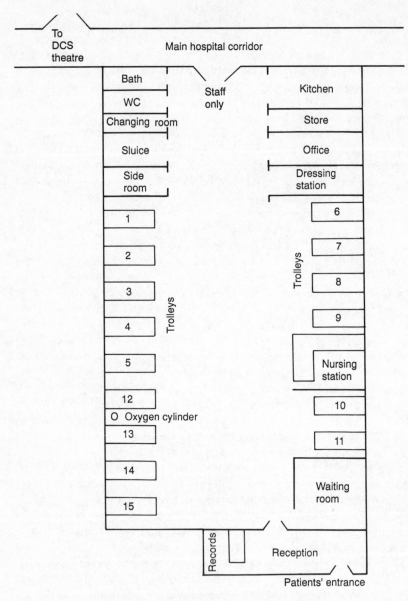

FIGURE 6.1 The day case surgery unit at General Hospital.

A day in the General Hospital DCS Unit

The layout of the day surgery ward is shown in Figure 6.1. The unit comprises a reception area, a Nightingale-style ward and, towards the far end of the unit, offices, rest room, sluice, etc. A door at this end leads to the main hospital concourse, and is situated almost directly opposite the entrance to the DCS theatre, one of the twin thoracic theatres, now re-designated. The main ward contains 15 trolley-beds, which can be wheeled directly to and from theatre; each bed is provided with an oxygen line and suction, and can be curtained off. The nursing station is centrally situated within this area. The DCS Unit is staffed by the clinical manager Dr F. (an anaesthetist and part-time manager), a ward sister, a staff nurse, a State Enrolled Nurse (SEN) and two nursing auxiliaries.

The DCS Unit is arranged so that access for patients is from the outside. The entrance to the unit from the hospital corridor is reserved for staff; patients are not permitted to use this entrance to the Unit, and those who do so are directed to the other end, which opens to the outside of the hospital. Patients are processed by a receptionist on arrival, and asked to sit in a waiting area until nursing staff are ready to allocate them to a trolley.

6.1
[8.07 a.m.] The first patient arrives at reception and, having been seen by the receptionist is taken by a nurse to trolley-bed 8. She sits on the edge of the bed, the curtains are drawn and the patient undresses and puts on a surgical gown.
[8.13 a.m.] As patients arrive they are asked to wait in the waiting area. They are called to reception, and checked in by the ward sister. A patient has arrived unexpectedly, having not confirmed his appointment. The Sister says 'Sorry, we had a place, but it's been filled. You'll have to starve next week'.
[8.17 a.m.] Patients in beds 9 and 4, accompanied by parents.
[8.25 a.m.] House doctor arrives, checks lists and goes to bed 2, now occupied.
[8.26 a.m.] Beds 3 and 10 occupied by patients.

Although patients had been scheduled to arrive over a period, there is a bottleneck in processing patients into their trolley-spaces, and patients are first taken to a waiting area from which they are subsequently taken by the nursing staff to their cubicle. Arrangements for post-operative collection are checked between reception and nursing staff.

6.2
[8.30 a.m.] Bed 4 patient is brought from the waiting area. A wait of 15 minutes has developed as patients are processed into their places. Patients are ticked off on a board at the nursing station, and details of transport home noted: 'Mother'; 'Mum staying'; 'We will phone'. Plastic identity bracelets are attached to patients once in bed.
[8.32 a.m.] Anaesthetist Dr R. sees patient in bed 6: 'How about if we don't put you to sleep?' Dr R. sees the patients in turn, some are given pre-medication, depending on the procedure, and the history of the patient.

[8.35 a.m.] Bed 5 patient arrives. Patients are scheduled for phased arrival up to 9.00 a.m.

[8.52 a.m.] Porter arrives, and wheels the patient in bed 1 to theatre. Manager Dr F. arrives and confers with Ward Sister.

Although the DCS unit has developed as an autonomous unit, its trolley area is sufficient to service day cases from other theatres at General. The Unit is servicing three lists today: an oral list (beds 1–5) in the designated theatre, an orthopaedic list in theatre S (beds 6–8), and a plastic list (beds 10–11). Patients are taken to the three theatres when called for. Previous to the creation of the DCS ward, day case patients were anomalous, and for example in plastic theatres, day patients were taken post-operatively to the recovery room. When they were waiting to be collected, they were put in wheelchairs just inside the entrance to the sterile corridor normally used to take patients on trolleys to and from the theatre by the portering staff. With the advent of the DCS ward, they could be taken back there when recovered from anaesthetic. In this sense, the DCS unit served as a *pseudo-ward*, where day patients would be based during their stay in the hospital.

Lists begin at 9 a.m., and soon patients are returning to the DCS Unit:

6.3
[*10.15 a.m. Patient 1 returns from recovery. The nursing staff are trained in recovery, and are detailed to ensure the patients are ready to leave at the appropriate time.*]
SISTER: We try not to give strong post-operative medication, and not necessarily a pre-med. We need to ensure a patient can get here and back without driving. If we aren't happy that a patient has recovered, or there is a problem with getting him home then they may have to be kept in.
RESEARCHER: How often does this happen?
AUXILIARY [*looking through records*]: Eight times this month . . . 26 since February [four months previous].

In the theatre designated for day case surgery, the routine of the list proceeds, fed by the pool of patients in the DCS Unit.

6.4
[*DCS Theatre: 11.05 a.m.; patient is brought into DCS theatre, having been anaesthetized after a 30-minute wait in the anaesthetic room. The operation begins – the removal of wires following a road traffic accident two weeks previously.*]
[11.15 a.m.] DR R. [anaesthetist]: Is it time for the next patient? [i.e. to have the porter bring the next patient to the anaesthetic room.]
MR P.: No. [*to researcher*] This is an ideal case for day surgery. It would be very painful under local anaesthesia, and time-consuming because we have to do it all the way round the jaw.
[*11.35 a.m. Jaw wires removed, Mr P. begins on the wires which have been inserted through the eyebrows. These cause considerable problems, and*

there is haemorrhaging, which causes adverse commentary from the
anaesthetist, and apologies from Mr P.]
[*11.45 a.m. First wire removed.*]
[*11.50 a.m. Second wire removed.*] MR P.: OK, we're sewing up now.
[11.52 a.m.] MR P. [*to anaesthetist*]: OK. [*Dr R. sends for next patient.*]
[*11.56 a.m. Patient is taken to recovery. Dr R. goes to the anaesthetic room*
and induces the next patient. There is a very smooth progress of patients
through the list.]

Meanwhile, patients are recovering in the Unit post-operatively. The early
morning rush is replaced by a much more tranquil routine of care, discharge and
administrative duties.

6.5
DCS Unit
[12.30 p.m.] Patient in bed 2 discharged. Relatives of other patients are
    waiting for decision on discharge, which is made by ward sister, after
    consultation with clinicians.
[12.40 p.m.] Sister, SEN and one auxiliary go to lunch, leaving staff nurse
    in control of unit.
[1.05 p.m.] The oral list is complete. Mr P. comes to the unit, and leaves
    some instructions with the staff nurse. Patients are discharged through-
    out the afternoon.
[4.40 p.m.] Unit closes.

The ethnographic data documented in this snapshot of the DCS Unit at General
indicates the relatively smooth processing of surgical patients through the Unit
and theatre. None of the disruption and 'inefficiency' reported in Chapter 5 was
witnessed. In the light of the analysis developed there, it might be hypothesized
that this is a consequence of the local managerial arrangements institutionalized
within the DCS Unit, which in some ways resolve the conflict between surgical
and managerial discourses. To evaluate the extent to which the day case model of
surgical healing is distinctive in terms of social processes, this case study will now
turn to the context in which DCS was implemented at General Hospital.

DCS at General Hospital: the background

As Gabbay and Francis (1988) point out, much has been published in the medical
journals upon the topic of day surgery over the past 20 years, with most reports
favouring an increase. Estimates of the amount of surgery possible on a day basis
vary from under a quarter to as much as half of all surgical cases. DCS is now
being conducted in designated units in many large hospitals, although the reality
is that the amount of DCS has not reached the levels suggested by its advocates
(Gabbay and Francis, p. 1249). In 1986, 710 000 day cases were conducted,

approximately one-fifth of all surgical cases (HMSO, 1988). The Commission on surgical services (Royal College of Surgeons of England, 1985) provided guidelines for DCS which amounted to an enthusiastic endorsement of it as a complementary system to conventional surgery, which would reduce waiting lists, reduce the costs of surgery, reduce disruption to patients' working and domestic life, and increase the proportion of consultant surgeons in the surgical cadre (RCSE, pp. 1–2).

This backdrop of interest within the profession, and the subsequent high profile creation of DCS units at two major centres of surgical excellence, was certainly a factor in developing an interest among surgeons at General in DCS, and as has been seen, a small proportion of the surgical case load was being conducted on a day basis, although without a designated unit. In early conversations with surgical informants, and a number anaesthetists who were interested in surgical management, the creation of the designated unit at General was assumed to be a consequence of this backdrop of enthusiasm within the profession. However, it subsequently transpired as a result of enquiries that the decision in November 198- to set up a working party with a brief to consider and plan a designated DCS unit, was management-led. Earlier that year, a policy document circulated at District Health Authority level set out a strategic planning brief for hospitals in the district. The re-organizations and rationalizations identified in this document as necessary in terms of efficient use of resources held, *inter alia*, implications for surgery at General Hospital. These principally arose as a consequence of the geographical location of General, in the north east of a large city served by two further general hospitals ('Western' and 'Southern'), each managed, for historical reasons, by a different district health authority. The significance of this proximity was twofold. Firstly, close comparisons were possible due to the similar sociodemographic characteristics of the populations served. Secondly, a degree of duplication of services in a number of specialties had arisen historically, and were now subject to rationalization. At General Hospital, the definition of 'general surgery' had been widening to include vascular surgery. The consequence had been a diminishing role for thoracic surgery at General, and a resulting under-utilization of services, including a twin theatre suite built to palatial proportions for a once-planned cardiac surgical service. By the mid-1980s, Western Hospital was in the process of creating a prestigious cardiac surgical unit. This centre of excellence would draw further work from thoracic surgery at General. The policy document identified this problem, but avoided a decision on closing thoracic surgery altogether:

6.6

EXPECTED CHANGES IN PRACTICE AND WORKLOAD . . . A number of options are being explored for the future of Thoracic Surgery. The minimum effect on the general Surgery Service will be the equivalent of the existing overlap with Thoracic Surgery. One option, though not the preferred option for the long term, allows the Thoracic Surgery centre to remain at [General] Hospital within a confederation of surgical specialties inclusive of General Surgery and others, it being obligatory for those concerned to recognise the complementary roles of Thoracic Surgery and General Surgery, to maintain an adequate level of service to meet the long term demand for Thoracic Surgery and to ensure the underutilised resource is redeployed to meet real need. . . . [General] Hospital will not provide a specialist Vascular Surgery Centre.

The consequences of these elements in the Strategic Plan were translated into a language of reality by the hospital's commissioning officer:

6.7

MANAGER H.: Thoracic surgery has become something of an anachronism. Much of the work is now done in general surgery, and operative intervention in the very elderly, for instance for carcinomas within the chest, is very questionable in terms of outcome and quality. So they [thoracic surgeons] are being squeezed.

This squeezing took the form of the closure of one of the three wards allocated to the sub-specialty, and re-allocation of some of the theatre time to other surgery. Thoracic surgery was prevented from being completely run down by the intervention of the Unit general manager, after a meeting the following July, when the thoracic surgeons argued that they had been rationalized as much as possible, according to Manager H. As will be seen, this change in emphasis had a consequence for the development of DCS at General, in that it freed ward and theatre facilities. However, it was admission data in the Strategic Plan which had the most immediate effect upon the creation of a DCS unit. The plan provided comparisons for the year of 1984 of the proportion of day surgery at General and its associated hospitals (5.3 per cent), with Western (17.6 per cent) and Southern (14.5 per cent), with the region as a whole (18.4 per cent) and for the whole of England (20.3 per cent). The Strategic plan commented:

6.8

A feature of the [General] Hospital services is the apparent very low proportion of work conducted on a day case basis, compared with other authorities. . . . The proportion of the workload carried out on a day case basis will rise to 20 per cent . . . an increasing number of referrals will be suitable for day case limits. . . . Special day case facilities or a special day case organization will be provided for a minimum of 700 day cases per annum. . . .

These *management-led* decisions were therefore the backcloth to the formation of a working party at General in late 198- with a brief to consider the creation of a designated DCS unit. The chair of the working party was consultant anaesthetist Dr F. (who later became clinical manager of the DCS unit), its membership comprised a consultant surgeon, another anaesthetist, the operating department and in-patient service managers, the Unit (i.e. General and its satellite hospitals) accountant and the Unit planner, and a physician involved with endoscopy. The working party invited submissions, and its existence was publicized within the Unit. A firm decision was made to go ahead with a designated DCS unit, and with the running-down of thoracic surgery, a ward was closed and refurbished to form the day case unit.

As was noted at the beginning of this chapter, it was particularly fortuitous that the period of field work roughly coincided with these moves towards a DCS unit. Consequently I was able to interview a number of the interested parties, some of whom were giving evidence to, or were members of the working party, at the very time when the changes were being implemented. These data should assist an analysis of the social processes which influence day surgery, and any differences from the traditional model, which has been the focus of this book.

Staff attitudes to DCS

Some informants were extremely positive about the possibility of more day surgery:

6.9

ORAL SURGEON MR P.: We seem to be ludicrously behind the times here. I have just done a case which could have been a day case. All orthodontics and soft tissue work, cases which only require a general anaesthetic because the patient is disturbed, could be done as day surgery. It would make no difference to me. The boys [house doctors] will be in to clerk the patient, and make sure he does not have a cold, check the right X-rays are there . . .

RESEARCHER: What will it mean in terms of making up a list?

MR P.: At the moment, we make up the list. With day case surgery, the administration will pull patients off a waiting list which will have been vetted by me as appropriate. At out-patients I will make an assessment, and will have to make sure they have a post-operative appointment – I'm not sure how that will work.

RESEARCHER: What are the advantages for you?

MR P.: I did not have the all-day list which I wanted. Now with the day case unit I will have. I had to cancel a Wednesday clinic, but the day case unit has given me the opportunity to get what I wanted. I can mix day case and non-day case patients, it does not matter one iota whether it is a day case or not in theatre, it makes no difference to the nursing staff. It may make a difference to my boys, who may have to come in at 8 a.m.

RESEARCHER: Will it mean you can do more cases?

MR P.: At the moment I do 16 operations a week on average. I cannot think about increased turnover, because we always get it wrong.

Mr P's enthusiasm was thus based upon the opportunity to streamline pre- and post-operative routines of the hospital to suit his preferences for particular techniques of surgery in particular cases. Once the Unit was opened, his enthusiasm was undiminished:

6.10

MR P.: It's terrific. I get two lists a week. Five patients on Friday, three or four on a Tuesday. I'm pushing the work through, a lot of minor stuff which is a money-waste to have in for two nights. I put the patients on the waiting list – it requires clinical acumen to decide who should be a day patient. If the procedure is technically quick that's better. Patient's who don't like local anaesthesia, but will take it because of the length of the waiting list, can now have a general. I suspect we have generated a lot of work.

This surgeon thus perceived the advantage in management terms – the efficient use of services, and the provision of appropriate treatment. He was not actually carrying out *more* surgery, rather he was carrying out 'better' surgery. These managerial arguments for DCS were considered in a more negative light by other informants. The anaesthetist Dr J. identified an unwelcome trend in moves towards DCS.

6.11

DR J.: The supposed enthusiasm for providing day surgery within existing facilities is part of the thirst for funding to reduce waiting lists. Administrators would say they only act on medical advice, but with the day surgery proposals, the decision has come from the top, as pressure to reduce the waiting list, even if it's inconvenient to people. Is this approach going to be applied to other areas of practice? . . . I am not convinced that there is enough work for a day case unit here.

Another anaesthetist who had doubts, perceiving DCS as a management-inspired model was Dr R. He remained unconvinced even after the DCS unit was running:

6.12

DR R.: Day case surgery is a religion; the point is to make patients better. We have to ensure that day case patients are not disadvantaged, and feel comfortable. Patients who come in for head and neck things get bashed around a lot. There's an idea that because it's teeth, it's minor – surgeons don't understand that there may be a great deal of bruising and pain. This patient is going to be black and blue afterwards.

This anaesthetist identified the high degree of managerial control of the routines, which sometimes lead to problems for clinicians:

6.13

DR R.: I want to get children put further down a day list, because they come in in a real hyped-up state, with Mum virtually hysterical. We will get them down the list, but it takes four weeks to get anything changed.

The anaesthetist who had developed the greatest enthusiasm for DCS was Dr F., who was to become chair of the working party, and eventually clinical manager of the DCS unit. The first interview with Dr F., nine months before the unit opened, despite being conducted in theatre during a list he was anaesthetizing, had the feeling of a meeting with management.

6.14

DR F.: Developing day surgery is a matter of resourcing and logistics. It does entail a change in surgical practice – but not so much in terms of technique as in patient management. The research that is needed concerns feasibility – what kind of surgery might be done, where it is to be done, and taking into account what day surgery is already being done, to consider ward design and operational policy. . . . Surgeons will only change if they are forced.

This latter remark may have been prescient as subsequently, in addition to the assignment of operating department manager Nurse F. to take day-to-day responsibility for both the DCS theatre and the ward, Dr F. was appointed as clinical manager of the DCS unit, reflecting the need for a clinician (rather than a manager) to negotiate with the surgeons to change hours of service and arrangements which had developed over a long historical period. As he himself noted in a second interview:

6.15

DR F.: Doctors don't like to be told what to do by administrators. So it's necessary to have some sort of interface between the doctors and the administration. I understand the doctors and can talk to them, and also have respect for the managers. It's down to personality.
RESEARCHER: What's it like being a manager?
DR F.: I've got a lay manager's job, which is quite nice. I go round and solve the problems, giving broad directives, seeing the nurses are happy, seeing colleagues and saying 'It can't be done'. When it comes to finance, I need advice from professional managers.

Commissioning manager H. during the planning of the Unit told of further antagonism from clinicians. The decision by the working party to set up a designated unit had met with considerable opposition from the thoracic surgeons – who were losing one of their two theatres as a consequence, and who eventually complained to the Unit General Manager that they would have to reduce their turnover of patients if squeezed further. There was also a submission from general surgeon, Mr L., in the form of a letter strongly opposing the proposal:

6.16

[*Letter from Mr L. to working party on DCS*] In terms of modern technology – both investigative and operative – it [a designated DCS unit] is an irrelevance, and in terms of bed usage it is out of date. It is undoubtedly of some use in a badly run team or organisation, but it is of no use in an efficient system. With modern technology, the accent on diagnosis falls on the out-patient clinics, and patients reach the ward fully worked up for surgery.

Therefore no beds are needed in any amount for investigations. Occasionally there is a need, but it is too small to be important. In terms of surgery, day beds make no difference if a team's time is already saturated with theatre work. Any good team uses its theatre time to a maximum, so additional day beds are an irrelevance.

Finally, a ward dealing with major surgery runs best if the pressure is off every now and then. This release is afforded by the 'day-case' and allows beds to be available for evening emergencies. Day beds become useful, where excellence is a rare bird.

This last submission is of some assistance in identifying the logic of opposition. Whereas the thoracic surgeons' complaints are easy to understand (loss of a theatre,. loss of a ward, probable downgrading of their influence in the hospital), Mr L's comments range arguments concerning the relationship between management and clinicians. Managerial commitment to DCS is 'out of date'. The surgical teams at General are already 'efficient', and effective in diagnosis. Spare beds allow for emergency surgery out-of-hours. 'Excellence' is an efficiency less concerned with management-inspired classification of patients between day unit and traditional in-patient treatment, but with the provision of appropriate clinical decisions.

Similar arguments were deconstructed at the end of Chapter 5, opposing management and clinical definitions of 'good' surgery. This submission demonstrates the antagonism that a perceived management-led innovation could provoke in a clinician in a particularly concise way. Even with the enthusiastic Mr P., this conflict of definitions gave him a nagging doubt:

6.17

MR P.: I'm not totally sure about the division of responsibility for patients between the day-case unit manager and the consultant surgeon. It's just a mini-doubt, but I would not expect the ward to discharge my patient at five o'clock without my say-so.

This doubt, articulated before the DCS Unit opened, was resolved by a procedure whereby the unit's sister called the surgeon when s/he considered the patient had recovered and could be discharged. If there was any doubt, the surgeon would visit the trolley-unit to make a decision.

These examples of opposition were regarded by Manager H. and Dr F. as isolated reaction, which would soon collapse once the Unit was in use. However, such opposition had not been resolved four months after the DCS Unit opened, as an interview with Dr F. demonstrated. Despite the availability of the unit, it had not been adopted for use by the surgeons as had been hoped.

6.18

DR F.: The problems are that we have not got a unique unit, with unique sessions – the unit supplies patients to different mixed lists. The surgeons are not involved in the Unit. The clinicians have to change the emphasis, but unless you push them, then there will be no change. We have provided the facility, so they will see it and decide to use it. On the other hand, the wards are delighted, not having to deal with day patients.

When the two general surgeons come, then there will be pressure on beds in the Unit – for instance for gastroscopies, ten on a list, under sedation. General surgery hasn't been enthusiastic, because there's nothing on the waiting list except varicose veins, and it's difficult to know whether they are suitable for day case surgery. A lot of 'lump and bump' is being done by plastic surgeons. Mr X. is very good at doing bat ears, but it's very boring. Day surgery routine operations are boring. Plastic surgery had money from the Waiting List Initiative, and we provided a facility for a day list – they say the waiting list is not a problem

The neurosurgeons are now doing micro-discs [a surgical procedure on the spinal column] on an out-patient basis. They are very determined to have a go at day case surgery, within the safety limits. I have my doubts, but I will encourage it to see if it works – there will be a lot of discomfort, and possible complications.

This summary, of aspirations and a few firm plans, suggests that surgeons at General had been slow to take up the challenge of day surgery, and that this was a consequence of compromising as a servicing facility for day cases on lists throughout the hospital. There is also a sense, which cannot really be examined without specific data, that the DCS Unit had been a top–down initiative which did not really match the kinds of surgery being done at General Hospital. The recognition that day surgery was 'boring' (a view that this observer would support) suggests that part of the claim to clinical judgement over list construction was partly a way of ensuring that an interesting mix of cases could be selected by surgeons.

Before moving to a discussion of the data, one final negative comment is worth documenting – from the Unit nursing staff:

6.19

STAFF NURSE S.: We don't see the patients ill, and then getting better. It's dissatisfying work here.

NURSE AUXILIARY: There's no time to fill in a care plan for an individual patient, so we can't give them appropriate care.

STAFF NURSE S.:We had a man yesterday, and because I hadn't got to know him even for a day, I couldn't give him the reassurance before the operation. I felt like a shopkeeper or a hairdresser. I'm looking forward to getting back to recovery.

The day case procedure had reduced any possibility of significant nursing care input into the surgical patient's stay in hospital. The recovery period and the preparation of the patient for surgery, where nursing staff have an input, had become little more than the management of bodies and the efficient use of spaces. The nursing role in DCS had been de-professionalized, against the prevailing trends in nursing (Stevens, 1979; Riehl and Roy, 1980; Webb, 1981). The use of a high proportion of auxiliary staff may reflect this down-grading of skills.

Discussion

It may be concluded that the introduction of a designated DCS Unit at General Hospital was not greeted with enthusiasm by surgeons. Four months after opening, only one surgeon was using the Unit for day lists, a number of others were mixing day cases and in-patients on lists in the DCS theatre. General surgery had not yet responded with any use of the facility. Mr P., the oral surgeon's reaons for using the Unit, are also of interest. As was noted above, he did not do more surgery as a consequence, but what he perceived as 'better' surgery. He liked the flexibility that the Unit provided, the opportunity to have the all-day list he had wanted for a long time, and to streamline pre- and post-operative arrangements to suit what he perceived as appropriate for his patients. His only qualm was over the possibility that he might lose the authority over discharge following surgery.

The vehement intervention by Mr L. denigrated day surgery on moral grounds – it is the opposite of excellence, of use only in inefficient surgical teams. In a well-run team (which therefore has no need of DCS) patients are diagnosed at out-patients and fully worked-up before admission. To use beds, even on a day basis, for patients who are only in for investigation, it itself inefficient and an indicator of poor diagnostic capability. Nor is quantity the measure of good surgery, good surgery is appropriate management which permits a balanced mixture of elective and emergency, busy and slack periods.

These two positions on DCS appear contradictory, but in fact, both are using the innovation as part of a wider discourse on clinical judgement. For Mr P., tangential aspects attracted him to the Unit: he would use it so he had the flexibility to do 'better' surgery in his perspective. For Mr L., DCS prevented this same flexibility because he would be unable to subvert this management-inspired concept in the way Mr P's specialty permitted him. For a general surgeon, day surgery would mean endless boring cases on a long list. For nurses, DCS means routine care with little human contact. Only for those for whom 'flexibility' is really a threat of 'inefficiency': management and those clinicians such as Dr F. who have adopted a quasi-managerial role, is DCS *per se* desirable. Reading the Royal College of Surgeons' document (1985) on DCS demonstrates that the arguments put forward in favour of day surgery are couched in primarily management concepts. Issues of clinical judgement and patient preference are both discounted, in favour of economic and efficiency-orientated arguments (RCSE, 1985, pp. 1–2):

> Many surgeons . . . have been concerned about the management of post-operative pain and the development of complications where the patient cannot be observed. They have often been unconvinced by the economic arguments. . . . It is now recognised, however, that resources will never be entirely adequate to support all that surgery has to offer, and that we must all be conscious of the need to make the most efficient use of what resources there are . . . day case surgery provides a useful facility and a very great convenience, appreciated by many patients. . . . Day case surgery can be effective in reducing waiting lists. . . . It can substitute for the unpredictable postponement involved in a waiting list, a planned and readily available provision of surgical care . . . day case surgery is in no way inferior to conventional admission for those techniques for which it is appropriate, indeed it is better.

Having made this assertion, the guidelines provide no evidence, but only details of how the policy may be implemented. The only support for day surgery comes in appendices devoted to queuing theory, and economic savings. A 300-word section on surgical teaching on day cases emphasizes the teaching potential in relation to planning clinical management, rather than any inherent clinical advantage of this form of surgery itself.

It would be most straightforward to append this section on DCS to Chapter 5, and its analysis of the different conceptions of what surgery is about held by management and surgeons. However, I would ask the reader to cast her/his mind back to Chapter 4, which identified the discourses used by surgeons on ward rounds. Three separate discourses all served to define patients as success stories of the surgical enterprise, and it was argued that these were important in resolving the paradox that surgery both heals and injures. In day surgery, as has been seen, there is little post-operative contact with patients. Even the nurses have a routinized role in relation to the patients, and post-operative care has been passed to relatives or friends (the presence of an informal carer is a major factor in deciding on DCS as an acceptable model for a surgical case). Discharge is a formality, and keeping a patient overnight is a mark of failure.

Coupled with the banality of the cases, DCS reduces surgical healing to a little more than a technical activity. The injurious character of the procedure is hidden only by dressings, not by the range of discourses which can be deployed in conventional surgery. It is not just the nurse who is de-professionalized, the surgeon is too (except where it allows *more* flexibility, as with Mr P.). All those cases in Chapter 3 which were claimed as success, which snatched victory from the jaws of defeat, are ruled out in DCS. It is a boring, routinized, managerial version of healing. It is unlikely to spawn distinction awards!

In Chapter 5 it was shown how, given a routine whereby patients are processed from admission to discharge, management acts to standardize this routine. Surgeons conflict with this routine when, for reasons of clinical judgement, they are not willing to accept the standard process with its rigidities and rules. The agreement between managers and clinicians at the level of policy is a consequence of clinicians trying to get a piece of the action through their 'advice'. In DCS, the routines have become that much more inflexible, and with a list building up, speed and 'efficiency' must be accepted as the rule. Management has organized, in the sense identified at the end of Chapter 5, as a response to a threat, closing off the possibility of alternative perspectives on the activity. DCS has instrumentalized the process of surgical healing. It is a managerial version of surgery, where a conveyor belt of patients pass through the surgical space. The surgeon has become a technician, a cog in the wheel of the clinic.

If physiological alteration were the only source of surgical power, then DCS would be a popular form of surgery, enabling processing of many patients. In fact, it *is* popular at General outside the designated unit, where the procedures are not routinized. The DCS unit reduces the opportunities for a surgeon to make judgements as to the disposal of patients post-operatively, to make those careful clinical decisions based on experience and judgement which allow her/him to do more than just wield a scalpel. That is all that is left to her/him, and as has been seen throughout this book, surgery is not just about cutting, it is about the legitimacy and authority to define someone who has been through surgery as 'healed'. In DCS that definition is consequential upon managerial arrangements, by which a patient is on a conveyor belt of surgery and discharge becomes a technicality, not the marker of the success of surgery.

I started this book talking about the rhetoric of surgery, the markers and the metonymies. Day surgery seems to denude the specialty of many of those rhetorics. Without them, perhaps surgery also loses its mystery, and with it some of the power which its techniques have supplied.

7 | COMMENTARY

The intention of this book has been to identify key elements in the discourses of surgeons, and of others involved in surgery, by which the authority of surgery as a clinical strategy is constituted. The ethnographic report has been organized around particular aspects of the surgical enterprise: sterile practice, movements of staff, patients and instruments, the relations between surgeons, anaesthetists and managers, the interactions that surgeons have on their wards, and the arrangements for day surgery. In all these areas, the data have been closely read, to seek out discontinuities, anomalies or apparent paradoxes – the 'gaps' which suggest to the analyst that discourse is serving to silence or cover over the strategies by which knowledge and hence power is constituted.

The first of the 'deconstructive' analyses to which these data was subjected, identified the paradoxical nature of sterile clothing, in particular the surgical mask, and led to a further discussion of how the aseptic practices of the operating theatre serve to guarantee that the dangerous business of surgery is not only 'safe', but seen to be safe. Asepsis acts not only as a bacteriological insurance, but also as a rhetorical marker of the process of surgical resection – as being something different to other assaults on the integrity of the body. For surgeons to possess a legitimacy for what they do (and hence a status other than that of a butcher or barber), these markers are clearly important, and this early analysis suggests a way of understanding how surgeons achieve and sustain their status and authority. This is a theme which is subsequently developed throughout the book. In Chapter 3, the fascinating relations between the two clinicians in the OT, the surgeon and the anaesthetist, and their separate perspectives on their patients moved the analysis to a clearer recognition of this paradox: that the 'healing' component of surgery is achieved only via a further 'injury'. The complexities of anaesthesia once again mark the former as the definition which is to be elevated in the equation. As that chapter was written, the phrase, 'the operation was a success but the patient died', and the surgeon's perspective of the patient who is 'doing better', even though s/he feels worse (Knowles, 1977) echoed in the text. The shared discourse on illness and fitness clarified the cultural acceptance of so-called 'heroic' surgery.

What the deconstructions of discourse enabled, by pointing up a possible contrary definition of the surgeon's activities, grounded not in a claim to heal, but the injury that s/he inflicts – a definition which is negated in order to assert surgical authority and prestige – was an understanding of how surgeons organize their discourses when (reported in Chapter 4) they come into contact with the other 'expert' on the body which they have acted on – the patient her/himself. These discourses are highly controlled and selective, enhancing the 'healing' definition, and down-grading the 'injury'. When it is impossible to sustain the former, discourse fails.

Chapter 5 focused on the management of surgery, and marked a deviation from this theme, to bring in the context within which surgeons do their work. Organization of surgery is the responsibility of management, but surgeons also like to 'organize' their work, around different priorities. The significance of a clinician's claim to professional judgement, and the autonomy to exercise it are in conflict with the managerial imperatives at the daily level of activity, and the consequence is the disruption of management-inspired routine. For the clinician, professionalism, flexibility and thoughtfulness are attributes to be prized, while for managers, and for non-clinical staff in the OT, these are threats to efficiency which need to be 'organized' out of the system. Deconstructions of these two contrary perspectives illustrates the conflict between 'routine' and clinical autonomy. Management discourse emphasizes the first as a means of gaining efficiency for the surgical enterprise, but this threatens to reduce the surgeon to a mere cog in a technical machine, processing patients from illness to health. Chapter 6, on day case surgery (DCS), illustrates this threat. DCS tends to reduce the surgical enterprise to one of mechanical processing of patients and is basically a managerial ploy intended to increase the efficient use of hospital resources. The data gathered indicate that clinical staff do not appreciate this emphasis. But the case of DCS also demonstrates *why* a 'technical' surgery is dissatisfying for surgeons. It strips away many of the possibilities for discursive marking of what is being done as a highly prized process – 'healing'. None of the controlled discourse recorded in the section on surgeons on the wards is available, the patients are selected for their 'routineness' and the unlikeliness that any serious loss of 'fitness' will result from surgery. Only the rhetorics of sterility remain, and these are observed conscientiously. Day surgery is unglamorous and unexciting. Observing DCS offered none of the *frisson* of danger that pervaded conventional surgery, however minor, it was as if all the uncertainty had been extruded, to be replaced with the humdrum routine of the conveyor belt.

The objective of this work has been the excavation of the methods by which surgical power is constituted in the everyday activities of surgery. What the deconstructions suggest is that this power cannot be sustained simply through the successful processing of patients through the surgical space. Surgery is not just a physiological equivalent to mending a machine. Because of the insult it causes, simple definitions of what counts as 'success' are not often immediately available, but instead depend upon socially accepted, shared perspectives upon how 'success' is to be judged. Surgery depends not only on its physiological processes, but also on a social process of re-classification of a person into a category called 'healed'.

I am not suggesting any underhand procedures on the part of surgeons here. What I am arguing is that from their own perspective, based on experience and intra-collegial agreement, surgeons are able to judge what counts as 'success'. But they also need to ensure that the same set of judgements are made by groups outside their own ranks – patients, public, politicians, anaesthetists, managers, etc. To do so is not straightforward, because these groups have other perspectives which could run quite contrary to the surgeons' own definitions (witness the conflict between managers and surgeons outlined in Chapters 5 and 6). What I have sought to demonstrate is how surgeons use discursive strategies in their interactions with these other groups. Deconstruction opens up these discourses to a reading which illustrates what is being negated – often contrary definitions which are just as 'valid' in an absolute sense. These alternative definitions threaten the only grounds by which a surgeon may legitimate her/his insult on others – that what s/he does is 'successful' as 'healing'.

So these discourses are the ways that surgeons persuade others to their 'truth', and by so doing constitute and sustain their authority to make those definitions. I will offer an example. Cancer specialists use various measures to define the seriousness of conditions; one of these is the notion of five-year survival. Certain procedures, including surgery, are justified by the statistical assessment that subsequent to the procedure there is a 40 per cent (or whatever) expectation of survival for five years. This statistic is in fact impossible to relate to any individual case, who at five years post-operative is either alive or dead. Nor does it offer a 'simple' mean survival period in years post-operatively. By couching this uncertainty in this particular formulation, an apparent 'success' rate for the procedure is constituted, and presumably on this basis patients are encouraged to opt for one procedure or another (McNeil, 1978). In the case of the various options for the surgical treatment of carcinoma of breast, these five-year survivals may influence a patient and her advisers in favour of an option, regardless of the qualitative effects the procedure may have. Two people in five survive to five years, all perhaps have suffered pain and emotional disturbance, how many would have survived to five years without the procedure? Yet the definition allows the surgeon her/his authority, and even when an individual patient does not make it to the five-year mark, that authority is not directly affected. The surgical 'truth' has been sustained by this discursive strategy, even if from an outside perspective the procedure failed. This is the reality of the ways discourse persuade people to 'truth', although the effects are rarely so dramatic.

No doubt a substantial part of the 'success' rate of surgery is entirely non-controversial, and I would not wish to give the impression that I am questioning this – I am not competent to judge either way. What I am saying is that surgical power is not something which is just a given, but that it is something achieved by social process. What is of interest in this formulation is the circularity of the process: because an actor is legitimated s/he can do certain activities such as surgery. The legitimacy also brings with it the power to define how we are to judge the outcome of these activities, and in turn the opportunity to make claims which serve to reproduce the legitimation. An interesting analogy is with the practices described by La Fontaine in a very different setting, the initiation of Gisu boys into manhood. She argues that the secret knowledge imparted by elder to initiand, and the subsequent acceptance by Gisu that the boys have become men, legitimates the elders as bearers of true knowledge. The point is not the initiation but the power of the elder and its (re-) constitution in every successful initiation rite (La Fontaine, 1977). It is worthy of note that such rites are surrounded by rhetorical markers (rituals), which demonstrate that what is being done is initiation rather than something commonplace.

What this commentary suggests is that one further act of deconstruction may be undertaken, over the source of legitimacy of surgical authority (which of course is another way of phrasing the question at the heart of this whole analysis – from whence do surgeons derive their power?). The data reported in this book supply the surgeon's own version – judgement, skill, flexibility, professionalism, etc. – all those attributes reported in earlier chapters when surgeons spoke of their commitments, by which they make claim to their capacities to heal. But the analysis in this book has argued that these commitments boil down to nothing other than discursive strategies constituted as part of a will to power, and capable of existence only as a negation to this will to power – to the narrowly defined interests concerned with privilege, control and exclusion which are the opposite pole of these attributes. The final negation is of power itself. The deconstructionist's role is to demonstrate that it is the will to power which is the dominant pole of the opposition. This is the truth which can never be spoken.

Is surgery special?

Three elements of surgery define it as different from almost all other clinical specialties: the degree of invasiveness, the use of anaesthetic techniques and its emphasis on sterility. For the ethnographer, distinctive features of a field are likely to be those that will become focuses, and in this book, they have indeed been among the 'nodes' around which deconstruction of discourse has been attempted. By so doing, these techniques have become privileged as *the* practices which mark the significance of what is being done in surgery, and the means by which surgeons can use discursive strategies to sustain their authority. However, surgery is one specialty among many in Western medicine, and all have high prestige and authority in this culture. So much of what has just been said about the need for surgeons to persuade to truth presumably also counts for other specialties. The power of obstetricians and gynaecologists over women's lives has rightly been a topic for feminist analyses (e.g. Macintyre, 1978; Arney and Neill, 1982), and Armstrong (1979, 1982, 1984) has documented the rise of various medical specialties. All specialties in Western medicine seek to possess the authority to heal, by definition, and it is therefore reasonable to predict that all will use discursive strategies to demonstrate their 'truth' as being the one others should follow. Indeed, there is a corpus of analysis in the sociology of health and illness to demonstrate this.

What I would suggest is 'special' about surgery is that it has accrued various methods of doing this particular brand of healing which can serve not only as technical procedures, but as rhetorical markers of what is being done. Unconsciousness, purity, the breaking of barriers between outside and inside the body, are all 'powerful', in the sense that they appear to be principles which avail themselves of multiple interpretation, which signify other things, stand for other things. To use a term which has appeared throughout this book, they are capable of serving as rhetorical markers. So aseptic routines mark that what is being done in resection is 'surgery' not 'butchery', anaesthetic judgements mark the possession by a patient of 'fitness' to resist the injury of surgery. Surgery as a specialty has accrued a proliferation of rhetorics, lacking in other specialties. This, I suggest is the social meaning of surgery, that its power is constituted through rhetorics about healing. Low-status specialties – for example those concerned with geriatrics or mental handicap – do not possess such rhetorical markers (although they may choose other markers, ones which do not relate to 'healing' at all). The authority and prestige of those who do surgery derives from the technologies (in the widest sense) which modern medicine has developed.

The great 'discovery' of Derrida (1978) was that signs do not signify their underlying concepts, but other signs. Culture, through language, builds up chains of signifiers; and as in a dictionary where one definition refers to other signs which in turn refer to others, culture is constituted by these patternings. Sub-cultures create chains which are not those of the principal culture; as industrial capitalism becomes dominated by information these chains become unstable, transitory, subject to the whim of the group. Rhetorics – metaphors, metonymies, hyperbole, etc – use this chaining to make connections that can serve particular interests. That is all that discourse does, but it is at the heart of human activities, because it can be used to raise certain definitions and diminish others.

The problem with the rhetorics of surgery is not that they enhance surgery, but that in so doing they deny other possibilities. Power exists only through the presence of the powerless. So long as the authority and prestige of surgery is unchallenged, those who have most to lose from decisions over what healing is – the patients – will continue to have options closed off. The purpose of this book has been to begin to open up those spaces.

Another voice

As far as I understand it, what the author has argued in this book is that surgery has a high degree of prestige, and its proponents have the authority to get on and do their work, because they have surrounded themselves with sets of practices which not only serve a technical function, but also help them to define what they do when they operate as a positive act of healing. The way in which this insight has been developed is by 'deconstructing' the data which the author collected.

This seems to be making something simple more complex than is necessary. When surgery did not have anaesthetics or aseptic techniques it was a barbaric, dangerous business. People died regularly under the surgeon's knife, and it was not surprising that surgeons were equated with barbers, and were regarded as far the inferiors of the sophisticated physicians. Modern medicine has made advances, and its progress towards understanding of bacteriology and pharmacology has allowed surgery to develop to a point where it can intervene in ways which were unimaginable a century ago. Surgeons have high prestige because they are very successful in improving the health of millions of people. And they have the authority to do it given to them by the General Medical Council, who in its wisdom judges that surgery is a legitimate way of performing clinical intervention in certain circumstances. If surgeons suddenly started killing most of their patients, they would soon lose both their authority and their prestige.

I also wonder if the author does not need to look at his own perspectives. He has deconstructed surgical discourses, but what about the text of this book: what would happen if that were deconstructed? The author has elevated social processes above physiology, and yet the social definition depends on the underlying physiology, doesn't it? I can deconstruct this: he is a sociologist and clearly he wants to show there is a social meaning to surgery or he would not have a book to write. We do not know enough about the author anyway. Why did he want to study surgery in the first place? How does it fit into his career objectives? Does he plan to do more work on surgery? These are the things we need to know.

A response from the author

This new voice makes some important points. I cannot assert that my version of the meaning of surgery is more valid than any other reading. Indeed, if there is a social meaning to surgery, as there surely must be given that it is an enterprise carried out by human beings, then it may not be the one developed in this book. The data which I collected have been reported in great detail, and while I have used it within a postmodern perspective, readers are free to use it in other ways as far as they are able. A feminist reading is certainly one which should be done, and perhaps a psychoanalytic reading would also open up some new positions. Nor have I attempted to argue that somehow the social meaning of surgery can stand apart from the biological significance of the intervention, only that when the latter tries to do without the former (as in day surgery), things start to fall apart.

As for my own commitments, I may have chosen to study surgery for all sorts of conscious and unconscious reasons, and I cannot really reconstruct them now as anything other than a gloss influenced by the context in which I am now writing these words. I certainly knew that it was new ground for a sociologist, and so I would be breaking into an area which had not been previously reported. I have no plans to do more work on surgery at present, as I want to spend some time looking at gynaecology, and in particular male gynaecologists. I wish to develop the insights of postmodern social theory for the sociology of health and illness, examining activities without the constraints of metanarratives of class or other 'social structural' factors.

Some propositions for policy

One value of the postmodern perspective is that it forces commitments into the open: it is no longer possible to pretend to be the neutral scientist. The implications of this study depend who you are, and where your interests lie. I will indulge my own prejudices briefly, to outline what I see as possibilities opened up by the analysis of the social meaning of surgery developed in this work.

1 Surgery's possession of techniques which act rhetorically to enhance its authority as a means of healing has implications for resourcing health care. The potential for changing priorities of health services in favour of prevention will be limited by the exemplar of surgery as a means of healing already-present disease. (*Note*: From another perspective, requests to government or appeals to the public for additional surgical facilities will be most successful where the planned procedures emphasize these rhetorical markers.)
2 The success of surgery at a physiological level should be subjected to detailed study. Concepts used to support surgical intervention such as five-year survival rates or 'remission', require scrutiny to evaluate the precise nature of surgical success. The natural history of particular surgical interventions should be studied to assess the methods by which surgery becomes a favoured form of treatment for particular conditions.
3 As a consequence of (2), proposals for 'de-coupling' physiological 'treatment' from social 'healing' in the surgical enterprise may be derived. It is suggested that they would benefit patients, clinical and nursing staff, by confining surgical intervention to physiology, extracting the rhetoric. Some possibilities include:
   - a massive increase in day case surgery
   - minor surgery in out-patients and GP surgeries
   - co-operative management of OT time on a daily basis between nursing staff, anaesthetists and surgeons
   - regular review and publication of success rates for different operative procedures, publication of surgical mortality rates and mishaps in surgical management, and a reduction in media coverage of surgery
   - discharge to no longer be the sole decision of the consultant surgeon

- increased recruitment of consultant surgeons among women, ethnic groups and disabled doctors
- an altered career pattern in surgery which de-emphasizes hierarchical power structures within the specialty and between surgery and other specialties, increases part-time appointments, and reduces merit awards in surgery in favour of preventive medicine
- support for 'consumerism' among the sick.

BIBLIOGRAPHY

Andrew, J. M. (1970). Recovery from surgery with and without preparatory instructions, *Journal of Personality & Social Psychology*, **15**, 223–6.

Armstrong, D. (1979). Child development and medical ontology, *Social Science & Medicine*, **13A**, 9.

Armstrong, D. (1982). The doctor–patient relationship 1930–1980. In Wright, P. and Treacher, A. (eds) *The Problem of Medical Knowledge*. Edinburgh: Edinburgh University Press.

Armstrong, D. (1984). The patient's view, *Social Science & Medicine*, **18**, 743–5.

Arney, W. R. and Neill, J. (1982). The location of pain in childbirth, natural childbirth and the transformation of obstetrics, *Sociology of Health & Illness*, **4**, 1–24.

Atkinson, P. (1981). *The Clinical Experience*. London: Gower.

Atkinson, P. (1990). *The Ethnographic Imagination*. London: Routledge.

Atkinson, P. and Heath, C. (eds) (1981). *Medical Work, Realities and Routines*. London: Gower.

Baudrillard, J. (1988). *Selected Writings*. Cambridge: Polity.

Beck, C. (1895). *Manual of Surgical Asepsis*. New York: W. B. Saunders.

Becker, H. S., Geer, B., Hughes, E. and Strauss, A. (1961). *Boys in White*. Chicago: Chicago University Press.

Bidwell, L. A. (1912). *Minor Surgery*. London: University of London.

Bloor, D. (1976). *Knowledge and Social Imagery*. London: Routledge & Kegan Paul.

Bloor, M. (1976). Professional autonomy and client exclusion. In Wadsworth, M. and Robinson, D. (eds) *Studies in Everyday Medical Life*. London: Martin Robertson.

Bocock, R. (1974). *Ritual in Industrial Society*. London: George Allen & Unwin.

Bosk, C. L. (1979). *Forgive and Remember. The Management of Medical Failure*. Chicago: Chicago University Press.

Bourdieu, P. (1986). *Distinction: A Social Critique of the Judgement of Taste*. London: Routledge & Kegan Paul.

Bourdieu, P. (1990). *In Other Words*. Cambridge: Polity.

Bowman, A. K. (1942). *The Life and Teaching of Sir William MacEwen*. London: William Hodge.

British Journal of Surgery (1914a). Sir Victor Horsley's clinic, *British Journal of Surgery*, 1, 515–17.

British Journal of Surgery (1914b). A visit to the clinic of Professor Garre at Bonn, *British Journal of Surgery*, 1, 695–8.

British Journal of Surgery (1915a). Sir John Bland-Sutton at the Middlesex Hospital, *British Journal of Surgery*, 2, 110–13.

British Journal of Surgery (1915b). Professor Von Eiselberg's clinic at Vienna, *British Journal of Surgery*, 2, 328–33.

British Journal of Surgery (1915c). The clinic of Sir Watson Cheyne, *British Journal of Surgery*, 2, 325–7.

Burkett, G. and Knafl, K. (1974). Judgement and decision-making in a surgical specialty, *Sociology of Work and Occupations*, 1, 82–109.

Casteneda, A. (1961). Historical development of the surgical mask, *Surgery*, 49, 423–8.

Churchill-Davidson, H. C. (1984). *A Practice of Anaesthesia*. London: Lloyd-Luke.

Claus, L. M. (1982). *The Growth of a Sociological Discipline*. Leuven: Catholic University of Leuven.

Collins, B. J. and Bibby, B. A. (1981). Calculating infection risk. In *Infection Control Nurses Association, 12th Annual Symposium*.

Cooper, R. and Burrell, G. (1988). Modernism, postmodernism and organisational analysis: an introduction, *Organisation Studies*, 9, 91–112.

Coser, R. L. (1958). Authority and decision making in a hospital, *American Sociological Review*, 23, 56–64.

Culler, J. (1983). *On Deconstruction*. London: Routledge & Kegan Paul.

Department of Health (1985). Distinction award-holders in England and Wales, *Health Trends*, 18, 92.

Derrida, J. (1978). *Writing and Difference*. Chicago: University of Chicago Press.

Dingwall, R., Rafferty, A. M. and Webster, C. (1988). *An Introduction to the Social History of Nursing*. London: Routledge.

Douglas, M. (1984). *Purity and Danger*. London: Routledge & Kegan Paul.

Doyal, L. (1979). *The Political Economy of Health*. London: Pluto Press.

Eisenberg, J. M., Kitz, D. and Webber, R. A. (1983). Developments of attitudes about sharing decision making, *Journal of Health & Social Behaviour*, 24, 85–90.

Elston, M-A. (1977). Women in the medical profession: whose problem? In Stacey, M., Reid, M., Heath, C. and Dingwall, R. (eds) *Health and the Division of Labour*. London: Croom Helm.

Emerson, J. (1970). Behaviour in private places: sustaining definitions of reality in gynecological examinations. In Dreitzel, H. P. (ed.) *Recent Sociology 2*. London: Macmillan.

Fisher, R. (1977). *Lord Lister*. London: Macdonald and Jane's.

Flax, J. (1990). *Thinking Fragments*. Berkeley: University of California Press.

Fletcher, V. S. (1977). A history of the operation gown and mask, *NATNews*, 14, 19–24.

Flood, A. B. and Scott, W. R. (1978). Professional power and professional effectiveness, *Journal of Health & Social Behaviour*, 19, 240–54.

Foucault, M. (1970). *The Order of Things*. London: Tavistock.

Foucault, M. (1976). *Birth of the Clinic*. London: Tavistock.

Foucault, M. (1979). *Discipline and Punish*. Harmondsworth: Peregrine.

Foucault, M. (1984). *The History of Sexuality. Part 1*. Harmondsworth: Peregrine.

Fox, N. J. (1988). Scientific theory choice and social structure: the case of Lister's antisepsis, humoral theory and asepsis, *History of Science*, **26**, 367–97.

Fox, N. J. (1991). Postmodernism, rationality and the evaluation of health care, *Sociological Review*, **39**, 709–44.

Freidson, E. (1970). *Profession of Medicine*. New York: Dodd Mead.

Gabbay, J. and Francis, L. (1988). How much day surgery? Delphic predictions, *British Medical Journal*, **297**, 1249–51.

Gennep, A. (1960). *Les Rites de Passage*. London: Routledge & Kegan Paul.

Gerster, A. G. (1888). *Aseptic and Antiseptic Surgery*. London: Baillière, Tindall and Cox.

Giddens, A. (1985). *The Constitution of Society*. Cambridge: Polity.

Glaser, B. and Strauss, A. (1970). *Awareness of Dying*. London: Weidenfeld and Nicolson.

Gluckman, M. (1962). 'Les rites de passage'. In Gluckman, M. (ed.) *Essays on the Ritual of Social Relations*. Manchester: Manchester University Press.

Goffman, E. (1959). *The Presentation of Self in Everyday Life*. London: Allen Lane.

Goffman, E. (1961). *Encounters*. Indianapolis: Bobbs Merrill.

Goffman, E. (1968). *Asylums*. Harmondsworth: Penguin.

Graham, H. (1984). *Women, Health and the Family*. London: Wheatsheaf.

Hammersley, M. (1990). What's wrong with ethnography? The myth of theoretical description, *Sociology*, **24**, 597–616.

Hartsfield, J. and Clopton, J. (1985). Reducing pre-surgical anxiety, *Social Science & Medicine*, **20**, 529.

Hewer, C. L. (1953). *Recent Advances in Anaesthesia and Analgesia*, 7th edn. Edinburgh: Churchill.

HMSO (1988). *Health and Personal Social Services Review*. London: HMSO.

Illich, I. (1975). *Medical Nemesis*. London: Calder and Bovars.

Johnston, M. (1980). Anxiety and surgical patients, *Physiological Medicine*, **10**, 145–52.

Karpf, A. (1988). *Doctoring the Media*. London: Routledge.

Katz, P. (1984). Ritual in the operating room, *Ethnology*, **20**, 335–50.

Kendall, P. C. (1979). Cognitive–behavioural and patient education: intervention in cardiac catheterization procedures, *Journal of Consulting & Clinical Psychology*, **47**, 49–58.

Knafl, K. and Burkett, G. (1975). Professional socialization in a surgical specialty: acquiring medical judgement, *Social Science & Medicine*, **9**, 397–404.

Knowles, J. (1977). *Doing Better and Feeling Worse*. New York: Norton.

La Fontaine, J. S. (1977). The power of rights, *Man*, **12**, 421–37.

Lockwood, C. B. (1896). *Aseptic Surgery*. Edinburgh: Pentland.

Lunn, J. N. and Mushin, W. W. (1982). *Mortality Associated with Anaesthesia*. London: Nuffield Hospitals Provincial Trust.

MacCormack, W. (1880). *Antiseptic Surgery*. London: Smith, Elder & Co.

Macintyre, S. J. (1978). The management of childbirth, *Social Science & Medicine*, **11**, 477–84.

McNeil, B. J. (1978). The fallacy of five-year survival in lung cancer, *New England Journal of Medicine*, **299**, 1397–401.

Matthews, A. and Ridgeway, V. (1981). Personality and surgical recovery: a review, *British Journal of Clinical Psychology*, **20**, 243–60.

Mitchell, J. M. (1945). The introduction of rubber gloves for use in surgical operations, *Annals of Surgery*, **122**, 902–4.

Mitchell, N. J. (1981). Theatre clothing as a means of reducing numbers of airborne organisms. In *Infection Control Nurses Association, 12th Annual Symposium*.

Mushin, W. W. (1948). *Anaesthesia for the Poor Risk*. Oxford: Blackwell.

Navarro, V. (1976). *Medicine under Capitalism*. New York: Prodist.

Navarro, V. (1978). *Class Struggle. The State and Medicine*. Oxford: Martin Robertson.

Navarro, V. (ed.) (1982). *Imperialism, Health and Medicine*. London: Pluto.

Oakley, A. (1980). *Women Confined*. Oxford: Martin Robertson.

Orr, N. (1981). Is a mask necessary in the operating theatre? *Annals of the Royal College of Surgeons*, **43**, 390–1.

Parker, M. (1990). Postmodernism and Organisational Analysis: A Contradiction in Terms? Paper presented at the British Sociological Association Conference, University of Surrey, April 1990.

Parsons, T. (1951). *The Social System*. New York: Free Press.

Prior, L. (1988). The architecture of the hospital, *British Journal of Sociology*, **39**, 86–113.

Rawlings, B. (1985). It's All their Fault: Communication Problems and their Consequences in a Hospital. Paper presented at BSA Medical Sociology Conference, University of York, September 1985.

Reynolds, M. (1978). No news is bad news: patients' views about communication in hospital, *British Medical Journal*, **1**, 1673–6.

Ridgeway, V. and Matthews, A. (1982). Psychological preparation for surgery, *British Journal of Clinical Psychology*, **21**, 271–80.

Riehl, J. P. and Roy, C. (eds) (1980). *Conceptual Models for Nursing Practice*. New York: Appleton-Century-Crofts.

Ritter, M. A. *et al.* (1975). The operating room environment as affected by people and the surgical face mask, *Clinical Orthopaedics*, **111**, 147–50.

Roberts, H. (1981). *Women, Health and Reproduction*. London: Routledge & Kegan Paul.

Rosengren, W. R. and DeVault, S. (1963). The sociology of time and space in an obstetrical hospital. In Freidson, E. (ed.) *The Hospital in Modern Society*. New York: Free Press.

Roth, J. (1963). *Timetables*. Indianapolis: Bobbs Merrill.

Royal College of Surgeons of England (1985). *Guidelines for Day Case Surgery*. London: RCSE.

Schimmelbusch, C. (1895). *Aseptic Treatment of Wounds*. London: Lewis.

Silverman, D. (1981). The child as a social object: Down's syndrome children in a paediatric cardiology clinic, *Sociology of Health & Illness*, **3**, 254–74.

Spencer, J. (1989). Anthropology as a kind of writing, *Man*, **24**, 145–64.

Stevens, B. J. (1979). *Nursing Theory*. Boston: Little, Brown & Co.

Stimson, G. (1976). General practitioners, trouble and types of patients. In Stacey, M. (ed.) *The Sociology of the NHS* (Sociological Review Monograph). Keele: University of Keele.

Strong, P. (1978). *The Ceremonial Order of the Clinic*. London: Routledge.

Strong, P. (1979). Sociological imperialism and the profession of medicine, *Social Science & Medicine*, **13A**, 199–215.

Travis, C. R. (1985). Medical decision making and elective surgery: the case of hysterectomy, *Risk Analysis*, **5**, 241–51.

Trostle, J. A. (1988). Medical compliance as an ideology, *Social Science & Medicine*, **27**, 1299–308.

Tuckett, D. (1985). *Meetings Between Experts*. London: Tavistock.

Turner, B. (1986). *The Body and Society*. Oxford: Blackwell.

Turner, V. (1968). *The Drums of Affliction*. Oxford: Clarendon Press.

Turner, V. (1969). *The Ritual Process*. London: Routledge & Kegan Paul.

Tyler, S. A. (1986). Postmodern ethnography. In Clifford, J. and Marcus, G. E. (eds) *Writing Culture: The Poetics and Politics of Ethnography*. Berkeley: University of California Press.

Waitzkin, H. (1983). *The Second Sickness*. New York: Free Press.

Wakeford, R. E. and Allery, L. (1986). Doctors attitudes, medical philosophy and political views, *British Medical Journal*, **292**, 1025–7.

Wakeford, R. E., Allery, L., Brook, P. and Ingleby, D. (1986). Characteristics of medical students wanting to be GPs, *Journal of the Royal College of General Practitioners*, **36**, 228–9.

Webb, C. (1981). Classification and framing: a sociological analysis of task centred nursing and the nursing process, *Journal of Advanced Nursing*, **6**, 369–76.

Weis, O. F. (1983). Anxiety reduction following post-operative analgesics, *Lancet*, **i**, 43.

Zerubavel, I. (1979). *Patterns of Time in Hospital Life*. Chicago: Chicago University Press.

Zola, I. K. (1972). Medicine as an institution of social control, *Sociological Review*, **20**, 487–504.

INDEX